Journey In Faith

One Woman's Inner Transformation

BY

POOJA RUPRELL

iUniverse, Inc.
New York Bloomington

iUniverse books may be ordered through booksellers or by contacting:

iUniverse
1663 Liberty Drive
Bloomington, IN 47403
www.iuniverse.com
1-800-Authors (1-800-288-4677)

ISBN: 978-1-4401-5416-4 (sc)
ISBN: 978-1-4401-5417-1 (ebook)
ISBN: 978-1-4401-5418-8 (dj)

Copyedited and proofread by Lana Okerlund

Printed in the United States of America

iUniverse rev. date: 10/12/2009

I dedicate this book to my mentor, Dr. Daisaku Ikeda,
third president of Soka Gakkai International,
poet, peace-builder, and author.
Thank you Sensei.

This effort is also dedicated to my parents,
Seema and Dhanraj.
I love you Mom and Dad.

Table of Contents

Introduction

"In Buddhism nothing happens by chance. Everything has a meaning."

— Dr. Daisaku Ikeda, *Discussions on Youth*

I am from the splendid and colorful land of India. I was born and brought up in the country's financial capital, Mumbai, where I stayed all my adult life until the day I married my husband, Jagdish Ruprell, in 1993 and moved to a city in the south of India called Chennai.

On February 3, 2006, Jag and I moved our family—son, Aman (then nine years old), and daughter, Reyna (then four and a half years old)—from Chennai to the gorgeous city of Vancouver, British Columbia, Canada. The decision to leave the country of our birth was one of the most difficult we have ever had to make. I vacillated for several years before I mustered all my courage to make the move.

Today, more than three years later, when I look back at all the upheavals that accompanied our journey to begin a new life in Canada, I feel a deep gratitude. Our new lifestyle and environment have very little similarity to the environment we came from, but had we not moved, I would have missed out on all the learning and growth I have been forced to embrace. Settling in a new country has required tenacity, resilience, wisdom, confidence, and, most of all, a lot of courage not to turn and go right back to where we came from.

I write this book with the intention of sharing my growth and learning with you. Choosing to follow my inner voice instead of paying blind attention to the opinions of others has served me well. Faced with career, housing, child care, and financial challenges, I pushed myself harder every time a well-wisher suggested I accept whatever came my way initially—and Canada supported me every time I wavered.

My anchor through all the upheavals I went through was my practice of Nichiren Buddhism, which I encountered in Mumbai in October 1998. Nichiren Daishonin was a thirteenth-century priest in Japan who founded what has come to be known as Nichiren Buddhism, a major school of Japanese Buddhism. Nichiren taught devotion to the *Lotus Sutra* and the chanting of *Nam-myoho-renge-kyo* as means to attain enlightenment.

As a follower of Nichiren Buddhism, I practice within an organization called Soka Gakkai International (SGI). SGI is a Buddhist network that actively supports peace, culture, and education through personal change and social contribution. It exists within 192 countries and is headquartered in Japan. The current president of SGI is Dr. Daisaku Ikeda, whom members refer to as Sensei or President Ikeda.

Throughout this book I refer to the teachings of Nichiren Daishonin and Dr. Ikeda. In fact, the cover illustration of a blue fly on a horse's tail is inspired by a popular letter Nichiren wrote to one of his disciples, in which he says: "A blue fly, if it clings to the tail of a thoroughbred horse, can travel ten thousand miles." I am that blue fly and the gorgeous stallion is my faith in Buddhism, without which I would never have gotten this far. I have found that whenever I connected my life goals to the Buddhist endeavor of peace and happiness for one and all, paths opened up where there were none.

However, my goal with this book is not to share theoretical knowledge about Nichiren Buddhism. As much as this faith has guided my own journey, the lessons I have learned along the way can be valuable to Buddhists and non-Buddhists alike. My intention in writing this memoir is to share my personal experiences, growth, and victories in the hope of offering support and encouragement of your own aspirations. I have held very little back in the stories drawn from every aspect of my life—my childhood, career, marriage, and motherhood—and as I developed the manuscript I gained further insights about myself. My journey of personal transformation is far from over.

I have soaked this book in deep prayer so it may somehow guide you toward what you are seeking to fulfill in your own life. I hope that by sharing my story I can contribute to your own growth, and to realizing the vision so many of us share in our hearts of a peaceful and united world.

Innumerable people have supported my journey in intentional or unintentional ways. To all of you I give my sincere appreciation for being there when I needed you. I can't begin to name every single person who has brought value to my life, but I know I am a better human being today because of the impact of all who have come to my aid. I have met many sincere and wonderful people, and some who have not been as kind—though even they exhibited some good qualities I was able to learn from when I chose to open my mind to the possibility. By sharing here all the lessons I have gleaned from many others, I hope to foster peace and joy.

Youthful Innocence

Being born in the massive and busy city of Mumbai, India, had a significant impact on my innocence and faith in the world. From a very young age, I learned I had to fight to survive.

I was born in one of the filthiest and most overcrowded areas of Mumbai. The community was close-knit, almost to the point of being intrusive. My family of four, my grandmother, and my dad's brother's family of six all shared a tiny two-bedroom house—eleven people, six of them growing boys and girls! To make things even cozier, my dad's sister's family of six lived right next door, and they were at our home more than they were at theirs.

My parents, older sister, and I slept in the attic, which had been converted into a bedroom. My grandmother would make the children living in our house line up at dinnertime, along with the four from my aunt's place next door. I don't know how the adults managed ten hyperactive and noisy children, with our voracious appetites, on a daily basis. We were not doing well financially, and growing up together was like living in a circus. There was always so much happening. The community and its people ensured there was never a dull moment in my life.

As the youngest, I was pampered by everyone. My favorite sibling was not my sister, who was seven years my senior, but my cousin Raj, who was three years older than me. I adored him. I spent every evening playing outdoors with my cousins and friends. We played hide-and-seek and other games until late into the night, refusing to come in until our parents practically dragged us in. In those moments, the squalor and poverty of our surroundings did not matter. We were children lost in the eternal innocence of play.

My best friend, Anna, lived right next door. Anna's mother committed suicide when Anna was very young. She burned herself to death, and the rumors were that she had done it to escape the abusive relationship she had with her husband. I did not trust Anna's father. He often screamed at my friend and her brother, and stumbled around our streets in an angry, drunken fog. He also beat his son mercilessly with a stick. The fury that emanated from every pore of his being scared me.

I was also frightened of a mentally imbalanced woman in our community. She always stood at her window, half-dressed, shouting at passersby. People in the community ignored her, but I couldn't. I would stare at her every time I went by her house, wanting to reach out to her but too scared to do it.

In the midst of these unsettled households and despite our crowded living conditions, my own family seemed blessed when I was small. My dad never beat us, and I don't remember him getting angry or raising his voice. He was my hero, and to me the finest gentleman in the community. The only times I saw him get upset were when his brother, my uncle, beat Raj—a frequent occurrence. When that happened, I would cry. It was unbearable for me to see the cousin I worshipped being hurt.

My dad didn't like the environment in our community, so at the first opportunity he bought a one-bedroom place in a different area. We moved in when I was five years old. Our new community was named Sunshine, and it was quieter, cleaner, and nicer than our old neighborhood.

The move was good for us as a family, but it took me a very long time to settle into my new life. I missed my cousins and asked constantly to be taken to see them. My sister and I changed schools, which was hard on me. My grades fell, and on some days, school was a nightmare. In Grade 3, one of my teachers slapped me across the face because she was frustrated with me and my inability to grasp her instructions. The force of her blow caused my glasses to fly halfway across the classroom. Teachers—as well as some of my close family members—often compared me to other more intelligent girls in the school, and I could not cope with that. I found myself losing heart in the face of the unhealthy competition and misplaced academic expectations. Believing I was average at best, I stopped trying. As long as I moved from one grade to the next, I was relieved.

As the days and years passed I continued to struggle with the rigid education system. I was taught to be honest, independent, and disciplined, but I also learned to repress my emotions. I grew up to hold set ideas about what was good and bad, right and wrong, and I learned to judge situations and people based on a very narrow set of perspectives and an inflexible outlook.

Nonetheless, I spent some of the best days of my life in Sunshine. I lived there in the same one-bedroom home with my parents until the day I got married. The community was peaceful and I made lifelong friendships that I continue to cherish.

We lived in a three-storey apartment building. Each floor had four apartments packed closely together, and the doors to most units would open each evening for regular gossiping sessions among the housewives. As a child, I looked forward to these sessions because it meant that all the kids would be let loose to play together. Every evening, I would run down the steps to play with my friends, rain or shine. As I grew older, I enjoyed playing with the boys as well, but was very conscious of the fact that not everyone approved of boys and girls hanging out together. It was a very conservative and closed environment. I would speak with boys only if I was sure no one was in close proximity.

It amuses me now to think of those secretive conversations. The disapproval of boy-girl interactions only served to create more mystery and excitement about the opposite sex. The convent where I was a student was for girls only, and the nuns would not allow us to speak with the boys in the convent across the compound wall. I was so frustrated with all the rules and regulations. I did not understand what everyone was trying to hide from me. Why did I have to stay away from boys? What was all the secrecy about?

I was excited to complete high school and start college. Though I continued to be an average student, I now felt like I was my own master. No one was monitoring every moment of my day, and the best part was that being friends with boys was allowed. I was like a bird let out of a cage. I was not yet very comfortable communicating with all these young men, but it was an exhilarating feeling to know I could speak to them if I wanted to. It was a good thing my curfew was 5 p.m. and that my mom was strict with me if I reached home even five minutes late; otherwise, I probably would have gone wild.

In my second year of college, when I was sixteen years old, I met Jag. He kept asking me out, and initially I refused, fearing the consequences of getting romantically involved with a boy. I thrived on his attention, though, and my desire to be with him finally melted my resistance. For the next seven years, Jag and I met secretly out of respect for my mom's feelings. My mom liked Jag and it was her confidence in him that prompted her to give us permission to go out, but ours was a conservative society, so she did not want anyone to find out. She was afraid my reputation would be tarnished forever if someone saw Jag and me together. Considering there were almost fifteen million people in the metropolitan area of Mumbai, what were the chances of that happening?

Of course, my mother never claimed to be the most logical person; she was emotional, overprotective, and paranoid, and she loved me to death. That being said, my parents were also open-minded. They knew about my love for Jag, and never stopped me from seeing him. They laid down the boundaries very clearly, but supported my decision. In fact, in the 1950s when arranged marriages were the norm in India, my parents had met at the age of fourteen and had fallen in love, and they were married in 1960. I guess that's what helped them to be understanding—they had been there.

Jag moved from Mumbai to Chennai soon after I completed my degree program and started working. Over the next two years, my parents met with Jag's family and arranged our wedding. By that time, I had made a new group of exciting friends who were much more adventurous than my college classmates had been. One night, as the month of my wedding to Jag approached, I lied to my parents, saying I was going to stay overnight at a friend's place. Instead, a group of us—boys and girls—went to a nightclub. This was my first experience of dazzling lights, a dance floor, and rocking music. I loved it. Dancing was always a passion of mine, so I went crazy that night and wished the morning would never come. We stayed out all night, and went for breakfast the next morning together with the boys on their noisy motorbikes. It was an unforgettable experience. I created memories that night that have lasted forever. The freedom of that time spent with my friends was a heady feeling.

Unanswered Questions

On the other side of the happiness and freedom I was experiencing as a young working woman in Mumbai was an increased awareness of an overpopulated city with huge economic and social differences.

Each morning when I took the public transit system to college, I had to push against a sea of travelers to board the bus. The aggressive ones got on the bus and the rest were forced to wait. My assertiveness was in direct proportion to my haste. In the overcrowded vehicle, with people hanging onto the open doors and overzealous men falling over me, I held onto a long safety pin, prepared to use it on anybody who touched me inappropriately.

Every day during the five years I traveled to and from college, my bus passed the streets of Dharavi, the largest slum in Mumbai. No matter how hard I tried to stay detached, I was often moved by the sad spectacle of poverty that stretched out before me: wailing babies lying neglected, little children crying for food, mothers with a baby in one hand and a begging bowl in the other, men beating women. Sometimes I used the local trains, and the scenes I witnessed on those days were no better. Lining the tracks were poor young children who did not have a chance to live the lives they deserved. They would climb into the train to beg or sell their wares. Some were as young as five or six years old.

Poverty, illiteracy, and corruption were staring me in the face every day in one form or another, but I could do nothing beyond hand out a few rupees. One day, I took a child into a bakery and bought her some goodies, but I was told by a well-meaning family friend who saw me that this was not what a normal girl from a nice family should be doing. I was warned to stay away from street people in the future, and I did. This was the reality of life in Mumbai, and I accepted it as such. Yet what I saw on my daily commute to and from work—especially the brutality against children—affected me greatly.

Abuse was also evident closer to home. I became friends with a girl named Devi in Grade 11, and I loved her like a sibling. We would hang out together all day, playing with her two little sisters. Devi's mother was like an angel to me; she was kind and gentle, and she loved having me over. Devi's father, on the other hand, was an alcoholic. Devi would share horror stories of her dad coming home in a drunken state to abuse his wife and children. Some nights he would not return home at all, and no one knew his whereabouts. On the nights that he did return home, Devi and her two sisters would try to stay out of his way, hugging and huddling together under a blanket. Devi spoke of her desire to run away from home several times.

She was my dearest friend. I wanted nothing more than for her to stay in school with me and be happy. We would go to the temple together and pray. At the age of sixteen, I believed there was someone bigger and mightier than all of us who would be able to change all our lives for the better. I prayed for Devi's dad to be kind to her and her sisters, but that was not to be. Instead, Devi's mother passed away and their family broke apart. Devi's dad left his three children to the mercy of some relatives and returned to his village in Kerala. Devi struggled to keep her family together, but eventually her sisters were sent off to their father and Devi disappeared from my life.

All of this had a very deep impact on me. For a long time, I tried to comprehend the cruelty and irresponsibility, the lack of care and love Devi had been subjected to. I was anguished and refused to make a new friend for quite some time. I was filled with questions. My search for these answers led me to Hindu temples and the community chapel, and I was drawn to Indian spiritual music.

The reason Devi and her circumstances affected me so deeply was that I had experienced alcoholism in my own life. My grandmother passed away when I was ten years old. After her death, my dad developed a serious drinking problem, and this caused a lot of suffering for my mother, sister, and me. In the initial stages, we ignored the subtle signs of my dad's dependence on alcohol. I didn't want to believe my dad, my hero, whom I loved so much, could succumb to the vice that had ruined so many other lives in the community.

Before any of us woke up to reality, my dad was completely addicted to alcohol and gambling. His personality transformed completely during the years of his addiction. He spent all his hard-earned money on drinking and gambling, and eventually stopped going to work completely. Many nights, as a young girl, I would stay near the window, unable to sleep, waiting for my dad to come home. I needed to hear his voice and know he was fine before I could let my defenses down and go to sleep.

Scenes from the past would flash through my young mind: days I had spent with my dad, laughing and being pampered by him; being brought home from a movie in a taxi at the age of eight because I refused to walk to the bus. Our community did not allow taxicabs inside and I would fall asleep on the way home, so my dad would have to carry me the last part of the route, huffing and puffing all the way. When he put me to bed he would pull his handkerchief from his pocket to wipe my feet. Then he would tuck me under my blanket and kiss me on the forehead. I would fall into a deep sleep, feeling secure and loved. When things changed, I was baffled at what had happened to my dad, and I was at a complete loss as to how to deal with it.

Our home environment strained, I spent many evenings at a neighbor's place. I was there to visit my friend Sneh, but always spent more time in the kitchen with her mother, Anju. She would bring me a chair to sit on while she made rotis (Indian bread) for the evening meal. She always listened to me attentively, and her kindness was unforgettable. I often ate with them and stayed at their place well past dinnertime. Watching them live a normal family life, I found happiness in their mundane daily activities. But on several occasions I saw Anju grow angry with Sneh if she did not do well in school. Anju would hit Sneh and scream at her, completely out of control. Again, the change of personality confused me terribly.

First my dad, the perfect gentleman, was changing personalities, and then Sneh's mom! What on earth caused these wonderful, loving people to act so violently at times? These experiences, and my constant fear that my father would hurt himself through his drinking, slowly but inevitably changed me as well. I began to find it harder to express myself, and communicating with others on a deeper level started to become extremely difficult for me.

I retreated within myself.

My mother was a housewife, and we had no source of income when my father refused to go back to work. In the heavily male-dominated Indian society, my mom did not have very many options. We lived off our meager savings and received some financial support from my dad's brother for some time.

Once I got married, my mom sold our home and moved into a much smaller place on the outskirts of Mumbai. She was constantly worried about where the money would come from for next month's groceries. No matter how hard she tried, my dad did not give up drinking. His liver was functioning at less than 50 percent due to all the abuse he had put it through. He was hospitalized several times, and each time the experience would frighten him. He would stop drinking, but then go back at it again within a few months. This went on endlessly, and the worst period was during my college years and early working life.

Seeing my mom suffer but unable to change the situation angered me. She was dependent on the male members of the family, and that dependence made me insecure. Indian society was, and continues to be, largely male-dominated. I resented this deeply. I failed to understand why men and women were treated so unequally, and the dowry system prevalent in my country made me extremely angry. Several of my college girlfriends were pulled out of school, halfway to completing their degrees, because their parents had found husbands for them. My friends wanted to study but were pushed toward marriage. These patriarchal attitudes seemed so unfair.

My friend Salma's parents persuaded her to quit school after Grade 12. She was doing well in school, and with a little encouragement could have been an honors student. But her parents wanted her to get married and settle down. They saw no point in her wasting hard-earned money on education when she would not be allowed to have a career. I was pained at the assumption that Salma would be happy to mold herself to the expectations of her husband and his family. It seemed grossly unfair that Salma's parents got to choose her future for her. It did not matter what she wanted; all that was important to her parents was that the man she had been arranged to marry wanted a housewife and not a career woman.

Was this justice? Why were women constantly being forced into roles others had chosen for them?

In my youth, I tried very hard to fulfill the expectations society had of me. But it hurt. I was unhappy because I wanted to be a career woman, and I could not imagine fitting into the typical role that everyone assumed was the natural progression of my life. My parents were broad-minded and protected me during the years I lived with them. They gave me the best education they could afford, and the freedom to follow my heart as much as possible. But once I left their home it seemed like a constant struggle to live a life of independence and follow my heart amid the viewpoints of the society I lived in. People around me expected me to change overnight and find satisfaction in being a good housewife who enjoyed nothing more than cooking and keeping a home. But that was not me! I wanted a career and freedom of choice. The people who loved me supported and understood me, but I was always trying to justify and validate my very existence. I was especially bothered by a number of judgmental, chauvinistic male co-workers whose opinions I gave undeserved importance.

I became frustrated within, fighting a war between my own desires and the expectations of others. To escape the reality of injustice and inequality everywhere I turned, I became a voracious reader. As a child I read fairy tales, but as I grew older my tastes changed to mystery and romance. I lost myself in romantic novels, imagining my knight in shining armor coming to rescue me from the cruel world. In my case, my knight in shining armor became my first Buddhist meeting many years later in October 1998. But there were more trials and tribulations before that sunny day arrived.

Encountering Hope

I left my parents' home when Jag and I got married and moved to Chennai. For the first year of our marriage, Jag and I lived with his sister and her two daughters.

Within a month of moving to Chennai, I got a job as a manager with a five-star hotel. I found it exciting and glamorous. I worked like crazy and was a star performer. My days were long and I was working an average of seventy hours per week, but I loved my job and I grew with the company at a very fast pace—until January 30, 1996, when my life came tumbling down around me after a motorbike accident.

I was on my motorbike at 11 p.m., returning home from an evening shift at the hotel. It had been a great evening at work and I was in high spirits, singing loudly to myself as I drove my bike through the dark, quiet streets. I started to lose myself in my song and went inward. Before I realized it, my bike veered slightly and hit the wall that divided the road with tremendous impact. I flew over the handlebars and hit the street with great force, sending unbelievable pain through my body. A colleague riding behind me jumped off his bike, waving desperately to stop a passing car. The driver and my colleague bundled me in the car and drove me to the hospital. I was fighting to remain conscious and was screaming in agony from a broken arm and leg.

After surgery, I was confined to a hospital bed for three months. I wallowed in self-pity and anger. I feared that I would never be able to run, dance, or move normally again. Being a highly active and fiercely independent person, I was tortured by the idea of physical dependence on other human beings. I felt my life spiralling downward.

I was completely unaware that hundreds of miles away in Mumbai, a large group of people were praying for my protection and good health. Jag's family had encountered the powerful life-transforming philosophy of Nichiren Daishonin's Buddhism, and were practicing it within Soka Gakkai International (SGI). SGI Mumbai members' collective prayers for my life, though unknown to me at the time, were the catalyst for me to encounter this life-transforming philosophy almost three years later.

After the accident, my life changed completely. Jag had been transferred to another city in India while I was recuperating in the hospital. When I was released, the home I had lived in was no longer available, since it had been provided by Jag's company. I had to move in with another family. I was completely immobile and dependent on others, and perhaps most painful of all, I was separated from my husband—the person I had come to this strange city for. We were able to be together only on weekends when Jag could make time from his hectic work schedule.

It took six months of healing and daily hospital visits to get back on my feet and return to work. I thought the worst was behind me and expected sanity to return to my existence, but I was wrong. The accident and the recovery process embittered me, and I found little joy in the things that had given me satisfaction prior to the accident. My career, which had been on a fast track and was once a great priority in my life, now gave me little excitement or joy. Instead, I was frustrated, bitter, and angry. My relationships with my loved ones became strained as I expected more tender loving care than what came my way, and I lacked the maturity to cope with the immense physical and mental stress. Close friends did not seem to have the time to spend with me, and it saddened me that they moved on so quickly in the few months it took me to recover. What's more, the financial debt from the accident did not allow me to quit my job and be with my husband, nor afford my own rental apartment. At the age of 27, I was an old, grudging, bitter, complaining woman. The girl in me had disappeared overnight and had been replaced by a sad and tired woman. I fell sick often, could not sleep, and was constantly restless.

To make things even more challenging, Jag and I conceived a child five months after my accident. My relationship with the family I was staying with was deteriorating, and in my fragile, pregnant, and over-emotional state, I started searching for an alternative place to live. I needed to secure a home that would provide me with some peace and serenity. A friend of mine, Megha, offered to help me out, inviting me to share her apartment for three months until I could make alternative arrangements. Relieved, I moved into her place with my one bag of possessions.

That experience turned out to be a nightmare. Every morning before I left for my twelve-hour workday at the hotel, Megha presented me with a long list of chores to do. Worse, she constantly complained and belittled me. There were mornings when I felt dizzy because the child I was carrying demanded nourishment, but I had no opportunity to sit down and satisfy my hunger. It didn't even occur to me to fight back. I took this as my due, because Megha had given me shelter when I needed it.

I accepted disrespect, injustice, and verbal abuse in other parts of my daily life as well—mostly from colleagues at work, but sometimes from close friends and family members I deeply cared for. Not that everyone mistreated me intentionally; some were accepting the exact same thing from others in their life and were merely passing it on to me. It was a vicious cycle that I, too, participated in unconsciously. This made me even more angry and resentful, but I lacked the awareness, conviction, wisdom, or courage to stand up for myself. I was constantly looking for approval from people around me and bending over backward to avoid conflict. This is unbelievable to me today, but that was my culture and upbringing. I had been raised to respect power, authority, position, and age, no questions asked. Angry about this, I turned inward instead of fighting with the system. I lacked the courage and confidence to find my own voice.

Eventually, Jag convinced his senior management to transfer him back to the city of Chennai because of my pregnancy. Happy that I would be with my husband once again, and now seven months pregnant, I found an apartment for us and moved in by myself while Jag wrapped up his work in Bangalore. This was a great relief for me. After a year of living out of a suitcase like a vagabond, I had a lovely two-bedroom home. I threw myself into setting up our new quarters with enthusiasm, joyously moving furniture around and climbing precarious ladders to store unnecessary items.

It is simply amazing that despite all the physical and emotional stress I was under, I had an uncomplicated pregnancy. In February 1997 I gave birth to a wonderful baby boy whom we named Aman, which means peace. Well, Aman was anything but peaceful. It was as if I had communicated all my pain to him while I had been carrying him. He came into the world angry. He cried a lot and would not sleep, and he did not let me sleep either. For someone who was already physically drained, this was an impossible situation. I felt emptier every day, and tried to make up for it by being aggressive and loud at times.

Fortunately, the hotel I worked for had an attached child care center for management staff, so I could take Aman to work with me. Still, my life dragged on. On the surface I seemed to be adapting, but I was only going through the motions of life. I was surrounded by noise and chaos, and I don't think I realized how empty, lonely, unhappy, and unfulfilled I felt.

When Aman was twenty months old, I decided to take a three-week break to visit my family in Mumbai. But even among my family I still felt disoriented and lost. The one thing that registered with me was that Aman quieted down every time my sister-in-law, Mala, sat down in front of her wooden altar to pray.

Mala practiced Buddhism, and on her altar was a scroll of paper that she seemed to be in deep communication with whilst rhythmically chanting the words *Nam-myoho-renge-kyo* aloud with open eyes. A constant stream of people came to chant with her. In my state of mind I found these frequent visitors inconvenient, but every time the chanting started, Aman stopped crying to listen quietly. Eventually it dawned on me that Aman was more peaceful when the chanting was going on, so I began to leave him in the space where it was happening. Stealing away to a nearby room, I would close my eyes to experience a few minutes of peace. In those moments of quiet, I think I enjoyed the rhythm of the chanting as much as Aman. The turmoil of the accident, the loss of my home, the fear of being pregnant and alone, and the stress of taking care of a little baby seemed, amid the calming sounds of the chanting, like a distant nightmare. It was only later when I read Richard Causton's book, *The Buddha in Daily Life*, that I was able to resolve the mystery of the effect of the chanting on Aman and me. Causton writes that once one chants *Nam-myoho-renge-kyo*, that single sound summons forth the Buddha nature inherent in all living beings. Clearly, the peace within me and my little baby was being evoked.

Something else that attracted me to Buddhism was a very noticeable change in Mala's behavior and attitude. She seemed calmer and happier than on previous occasions when I had interacted with her. She seemed more at peace with herself and her surroundings. I figured it had something to do with her prayers. When I asked Mala, she explained that her Buddhist chant meant "I dedicate myself to the law of cause and effect." From the moment she started to pray, Mala no longer believed herself to be a victim of circumstances. Instead, she believed that her present was the result of causes she had made in the past, and that her future would be determined by the causes she made in the present. As a result, she tried to create value in her own life and the lives of others in some little way every day.

My sister-in-law's explanation made complete and logical sense to me. What appealed to me most was that the philosophy she was practicing was full of hope, and had enabled her to move forward with tremendous courage. She did not have an easy life, but she was taking full responsibility to make her dreams come true. Human revolution—a concept in Nichiren Buddhism that refers to positive internal changes within a human being as they continue to chant—would take some time for me to understand, but for now, the peace and vibrant energy that the chanting evoked pulled me to it. Without my completely understanding the words, the process, or the philosophy, something within me was softening and opening up.

A New Beginning

A few days into my visit to Mumbai, Jag's cousin Jiya invited me to attend a Buddhist meeting. On impulse, I decided to accept, thinking I would have a few minutes to experience some quiet and peace instead of the constant hurried activity my life had become. Little did I know that this day would become the catalyst for many of the positive changes I would later make in my life.

The meeting was unlike anything I had experienced. About thirty people were packed into a tiny room, all chanting *Nam-myoho-renge-kyo* in the now-familiar rhythm of galloping horses. The sound of the vigorous chanting released all the stress within me. I felt the tension leaving my body, and I rested my head against the wall behind me, totally relaxed and comfortable. For the first time in over two years, I fell asleep without having to count to ten thousand sheep in my head.

I awoke when the chanting ended and a discussion on Buddhism began. I didn't understand a single word of the dialogue, but I was struck by the sincerity of the members and their unconditional acceptance of a complete stranger in their midst. The leader had a powerful voice that penetrated my emotional haze. I went home full of questions, which Mala enthusiastically answered. She gave me some reading material and taught me about the daily morning and evening recitation of passages of the *Lotus Sutra*. This recitation is known as *gongyo*, which literally means assiduous practice. I also started chanting *Nam-myoho-renge-kyo*.

It made me feel complete—in rhythm with myself like I had never felt before.

After returning from my vacation, I started looking for people practicing this Buddhist philosophy in Chennai. I had been told by the people I'd met in Mumbai that practitioners could be found all over India, the U.S., and many other countries.

I connected to the local organization and soon discovered a network of people who were happy to support me by picking me up and driving me to meetings, or coming by my home to chant with and encourage me. They treated me like a newborn baby who needed protection. Their kindness touched me and completely won me over. Within a month I was a full-fledged member, dedicating a couple of days every month to meeting with my new friends, chanting, studying, and just simply connecting heart to heart with other members. I found these new connections to be open and trusting. No one put any pressure on me; I was just naturally drawn to the vibrant energy surrounding the members and the fun they seemed to have practicing together. It was as if they had a very clear life purpose dedicated to bringing happiness to themselves and others, and this inspired me tremendously.

Though I was introduced to Buddhism through Jag's family, Jag initially did not seem interested in being part of it, and I respected his decision. He was eventually drawn to the practice in the same way that I was: members started coming to our home, and the joy they spread aroused his curiosity until he began to experiment with chanting and prayer more than a year later.

Besides learning how to chant, I also learned by heart the morning and evening prayers. I performed them diligently, no matter what time I returned home from my job at the hotel. Since I worked evening shifts and almost seventy hours every week, there were days when I did not make it home until 1 a.m., but I would do my evening prayers despite the fatigue. My commitment to Buddhism surprised me greatly, yet it felt as natural to me as breathing.

The Buddhist prayers are in Chinese and I did not understand the language, yet something within me was so responsive to them that I couldn't help myself. I am a Hindu by birth, and I often went to the Hindu temple while growing up. I also studied in a Catholic convent, and I loved going to the school's chapel. I grew up to believe in the power of all religions, but I was never committed to regular prayer. My parents had never forced religion on me either. I had been free to follow my heart and respond to my feelings where prayer was concerned.

Maybe that is why I felt an instant connection to this philosophy. Chanting *Nam-myoho-renge-kyo* gave me a sense of freedom and belonging like nothing else had. And the strangest thing was that it brought me closer to the religion of my birth. Today I know more Hindu prayers than I did ten years ago.

I absorbed Buddhism as a way of life more than a religion. I studied the writings of Nichiren Daishonin and Dr. Daisaku Ikeda voraciously, and the more I learned, the deeper my faith became. "Earthly desires are enlightenment," I was told, and I absolutely loved the message. As long as I was not hurting someone else, I was free to ask for the fulfillment of my desires—a car, the perfect job, a beautiful home—through the power of my prayers. That theory completely swept me off my feet. Even though I had come into the philosophy seeking hope, harmony, and peace, I was not quite ready to let go of my material comforts.

The word *enlightenment* no longer frightened me. I had always associated enlightenment with monks sitting on top of the Himalayas, spending their lives in meditation and living off plants—not a very appealing prospect. When I came across the meaning of enlightenment in the compilation of Nichiren Daishonin's letters to his disciples, it seemed attainable and sustainable to me. "Enlightenment is not a mystical or transcendental state," wrote the unidentified author of the book's introduction. "Rather, it is a condition in which one enjoys the highest wisdom, vitality, good fortune, confidence, and other positive qualities, and in which one finds fulfillment in one's daily activities and comes to understand one's purpose in being alive."

Gradually, I understood that the power of this philosophy was immense and could lead to bigger things than cars and homes. The focus of my chanting began to expand from my own personal benefits to the growth and happiness of others. I found that whenever a friend was facing a problem, I was able to resist chanting for myself and dedicate my prayers toward my friend's concerns instead. Initially I had to remind myself to do this, but it eventually became quite natural. Though I still occasionally prayed for my own material benefits, praying for others became more effortless. I soon discovered that my prayers could encompass the whole world.

Testing the Power

Buddhism believes in the interdependence of all human beings. This means that we cannot stay unaffected by what is happening in the rest of the world. I used to think I had no role to play in issues that did not affect me personally. I was a victim of this thought process while I was growing up and saw the poor and hungry children on the streets of Dharavi. I also exhibited this attitude in the year 1993, when a series of thirteen bomb blasts rocked Mumbai.

I lost a good friend, Vinay, in that horrible event. Both of us were part of a close-knit group for three years in the early 1990s when we went to school together for a professional certification in computer programming. I had absolutely no aptitude for programming, but Vinay was the star performer in the group. All of us would seek his help before an exam. He was so skilled that he was offered a job with the institute we were training at. He had grand dreams of going to America and making a future there.

During those years, every male I studied with had the burning ambition of working in the U.S. Vinay worked toward that goal for several years without much success, but he was persistent. He was at the passport office in Mumbai, along with his younger brother and uncle, when the blast killed all three of them. When the news reached me, I went with my friends to his parents' home. I looked around for his mother to extend my condolences. I spotted her huddled on the floor in the corner of the room, her arms hugging her knees tightly to her chest.

There were no tears, just a stoic expression on her face. I stood there frozen with fury at the senseless deaths and shattered lives. How were any of these people to blame for the religious war that caused these acts of barbarism? Over and over again, I asked myself in anguish if we were all just helpless pawns in a global power struggle—yet I did nothing.

After discovering Buddhism, I found it hard to seek peace only for myself in an environment where others were in intense suffering and pain, without making an effort to reach out on their behalves. My first opportunity to witness the power of my Buddhist prayers arose within three months of beginning my practice. My close friend Asha, who had worked with me at the hotel for five years, was fired from her job. She was heartbroken, and she needed to find a job immediately to survive. In India, people don't get fired easily. Significant social stigma is attached to being dismissed, so Asha was afraid to tell her family about what had happened.

I suggested she chant *Nam-myoho-renge-kyo* as a means of finding a positive way out of her situation. I started to wake up early every morning at 6 a.m. to pray for her too. Within a couple of weeks she had another position with a bigger organization, a better job profile, a more prestigious title, and more money. This experience strengthened my faith further.

I also introduced my mother to chanting so she could help my dad overcome his addiction. I had barely been chanting for a day when I spoke to my mother about it and suggested she try it. She had been suffering for over fifteen years, so she accepted my suggestion without question. She began to chant earnestly, and made an effort to attend as many Buddhist meetings as she could despite having to travel long distances on the overcrowded public transportation system. She spoke to several senior leaders and sought guidance about her financial problems and the issues with my dad. I supported her with my prayers, first from Chennai and then from Vancouver after Jag and I relocated our family there. Three years ago, my father finally gave up drinking.

My parents visited Vancouver in 2008, spending two months with my family. This was my parents' first vacation in twenty years, and I felt honored to show them my new city. Looking at it through their eyes was a humbling experience. My dad's childlike joy when I bought him a latte, his excitement in shopping with me at Costco, and his curious questions about almost everything were adorable. Many a day he and Aman would venture out on the bus to the shopping malls, and it was hard to figure out who was the child in this twosome when I came home to their excited chatter in the evenings. Joyful tears would blur my vision.

From the time I first moved to Canada, it was my earnest prayer that my parents would make the trip and give me an opportunity to show my gratitude to them. No matter how much I do for them, I will never be able to repay their love, care, and support of me, despite all their difficulties. This visit was just a drop in the ocean.

It took over twenty years for us to change our family karma, and several years of chanting *Nam-myoho-renge-kyo*. I could have changed this situation much earlier if I had been consistent in my prayers for my dad, but I was not. Every time he improved even a little, I would move on to something else in my life that I needed to change. I now understand how much commitment it can take to make a positive change, and the shift in our family karma shows me that nothing is impossible.

Sara, one of my colleagues at the hotel, was the next person I introduced to *Nam-myoho-renge-kyo*. As I got to know Sara and she shared some of her struggles with me, I spoke to her about Buddhism. Although she took up the practice seemingly quickly, she provided some of my most challenging, but also most rewarding, experiences. Initially, she would yawn, bored with chanting. She challenged me with a zillion questions, which forced me to study and develop a deeper understanding of the faith. It was as if she was waiting for me to give an illogical and unconvincing answer so she could stop chanting. She fluctuated in her practice for over two years, sometimes high-spirited and at other times filled with doubt.

Sara loved dancing and singing, and I encouraged her to take part in the cultural performances at Buddhist meetings as an avenue to help her deepen her connection. A natural performer, Sara basked in the attention of the audience. Her serious connection to Buddhism finally occurred when other young women made great efforts to support her and share their experiences with her. They picked her up and drove her to study meetings—and once Sara began attending these sessions, there was a complete shift in the way she practiced. Sara would study

Buddhist writings together with another young woman named Matty, who has touched my life greatly as well. They would read aloud together line by line. I found this strange at that point in time, but when I saw how Sara's life progressed as a result of her newfound wisdom, I realized how this was helping her.

Sara's life blossomed like the lotus flower because of her sincere efforts to connect to newer members and her contributions at every Buddhist meeting. Before embracing the practice, she struggled to make ends meet and support her mom and younger sister financially. She was forced to move away from home to make a career for herself, and I know she missed her family intensely at times. But through her focused study, she grew to the point where she was able to meet the man of her dreams, help her younger sister attend university, and finally reunite her family. I am humbled at her courage, and at the same time am proud to have been the catalyst of her life's transformation.

Deepening My Faith

Over the first few months of discovering Buddhism, I experienced the joy of chanting *Nam-myoho-renge-kyo*, and I appreciated the support of my new friends in faith. They became my champions. Senior members visited me at home and made every effort to help me connect with the philosophy. They taught me to fight every defeat in my life, big or small, through the power of prayer.

A leader named Bina was assigned to take care of me. She visited me regularly, and when she asked if we could chant together I very willingly settled down to do so for ten minutes. That was the most I could sustain in the initial months. Well, I soon found out that Bina's definition of chanting differed greatly from mine.

Expecting to stop after ten minutes, I tried catching her attention, but she was completely focused and made absolutely no movement. I must have changed position every two minutes, looking at her each time in the hope of signaling my need to stop—but to no avail. I finally gave up; I let her chant for as long as she could and just tried to keep pace with her. She was quite firm with me, yet so compassionate that I did not mind her firmness at all. She was very clear about what direction she wanted my Buddhist practice to take, and it was from her that I learned the art of taking responsibility for other members.

The essence of Buddhism lies in reaching out to one another and supporting our friends through the power of prayer when needed, and this was exactly the spirit with which Bina nurtured me. She visited me with the intention of chanting for my happiness and growth. Bina had her own challenges to cope with professionally and personally, yet she made time to encourage me. I sensed she was praying sincerely for me, and her prayers helped me open up and connect with her. In a very short time, she became a friend I could confide and trust in. I followed Bina's example, and whenever I prayed for others, my own life opened up further to good fortune.

Bina often picked me up for study meetings at her place. She would share her understanding of Buddhist writings, and always encouraged me to come prepared for the study so I could share as well. I've always liked reading and enjoy many genres—fiction, romance, fantasy, and self-help—so adding Buddhist study to my list was not difficult at all. I soon found that my new friends read and studied in a very organized and sustained manner. I enjoyed the discipline as much as the knowledge that Buddhist study meetings brought to my life.

I found particular solace in the writings of Nichiren Daishonin. His letters to his disciples have been a guiding light in my life. I do not understand everything he wrote, but with effort I have come to understand the heart of the letters and how they can relate to my life and attitude. They have helped me become a better human being and understand the Buddhist philosophy in greater depth.

I used to be quite a short-tempered and impatient person, always keeping so many emotions bottled up that when I let go, I lost all control of myself and reacted like a trapped, wounded animal. Within a few minutes of my outburst, I would start to feel ashamed about my behavior, but the damage had been done. The distress these episodes generated lasted for hours—sometimes even days—and made me miserable.

I was not always like this. I don't know exactly when so much anger developed within me or why I responded to life events so negatively, but it seemed connected to the agonizing experiences of my youth. The insecurities of growing up with low self-esteem as an underperforming student, uncertainty of my self-worth as a woman, and fear that I would be pushed into doing something against my will—all of these powerful feelings made me desperate to stay in control of my life, and suspicious of the individuals around me.

Anger made me behave in a manner that was most unbecoming and unlike my true self. I badly wanted to change this uncontrollable flame of fury within me. In my childhood I had witnessed how anger could change a perfectly charming individual into someone barbaric—and now this was me. I felt like a terrible human being, and that all the compassion I was feeling for others was hypocritical. Where was my compassion toward the people I was hurting, including myself?

It was the following lines from one of Nichiren's letters to his disciples that made me aware I needed to change this aspect of my personality so I could be at peace: "But you should know that the heavenly gods will not protect a short-tempered person, however important they may think he or she is." This motivated me to look at the negative aspects of my behavior and embark on my own human revolution. The result has been the most precious gift of practicing Buddhism.

Soon, my life was about much more than moving from one material desire to the next. I started to analyze my behavior, attitude, and responses, and think about what kind of person I wanted to be instead of focusing solely on the next fancy car I wanted to drive. I began to think I could be happy regardless of whether I was able to achieve my material goals, because those were never-ending.

As I interacted with my Buddhist friends, I kept receiving wake-up calls like this. All the opportunities I needed to become a more contributive human being kept finding their way into my life, forcing me to expand my learning. I changed in so many ways. From living most of my life hiding in the back rows, trying to make sure no one noticed me, I started to speak up and share my thoughts and ideas. From believing I had nothing of value to say to people, I began speaking from my heart to encourage other human beings. Sharing my life experiences at Buddhist gatherings honed my communication skills and vastly improved my self-esteem. I began to believe in myself a little more every day.

Jumping into every Buddhist activity became a habit. I stopped over-thinking everything and just followed my heart. As I prepared for and participated in song practices, study meetings, or other events, I avoided self-analysis and let myself respond naturally to the joy of being around a group of happy, smiling people who cherished me without knowing much about me. Their unconditional acceptance of me became another lifeline in my journey of growth.

When I first encountered Buddhism, I was a bitter, tired, defeated person. The saddest part was that I thought I had nothing to offer to anyone. I believed all the limiting messages I had been taught about myself, my intelligence, and the role of women in society. How wrong I was!

A Mother's Victory

After encountering Buddhism, life became a more enjoyable journey. I grew in all aspects of my being. Motherhood, especially, came more naturally. Aman became the center of my world. He had the most charming, naughty smile, and eyes that lit up every time he saw me. He would race unsteadily toward me for a hug, laughing all the way and refusing to let go after. Aman always wanted to play, and the fact that he had no one to play with was something he did not appreciate. He had an inborn protective instinct and was always running after other people's little children. All the younger children in the day care adored Aman and his creative ideas of play. He enjoyed being their leader and, to this day, he continues to have an effortless and spontaneous connection with children younger than himself.

It was Aman's love and desire for a sibling that prompted Jag and me to think of having another child. I conceived our second baby in January 2001. From the very first month, my pregnancy was fraught with issues. It was the complete opposite of my experience with Aman. I had massive attacks of breathlessness and absolutely no appetite. I was tired and my heart seemed to beat too fast and too hard. I struggled to do my prayers in the morning because I was short of breath.

In the second month, I fell very sick and contracted a virus known as herpes zoster, the same virus that causes chicken pox. I developed painful boils on my right arm. Because I was pregnant, my gynecologist advised me against taking any internal medication. Three months into the pregnancy, I recovered from the virus and went for my first scan. The scan results showed a small tumor in the brain of the child in my womb, and I was advised to have another scan within two weeks. My gynecologist hoped the tumor would resolve itself, but the second scan showed the same results. I was advised to have amniocentesis, a painful process in which a physician extracts fluid from the abdomen and tests it for deficiencies.

After a few weeks of having the procedure, my doctor called to ask me to come in to her office to discuss the results. I prayed feverishly before the doctor's visit for the protection of my unborn child—but to no avail.

The doctor informed us that our unborn baby boy (I called him Adil) had Down syndrome. If born, he would suffer greatly. My gynecologist recommended an abortion and warned us against another delivery, explaining there was a high probability any child I conceived would have the same syndrome. After five months of pregnancy, I was admitted into the hospital to go through induced labor and the death of my child. Because I was so far along in the pregnancy and the child was already so big, there was no other way to abort him. I spent that whole night crying at my inability to save this child I had wanted so badly. My mind could not comprehend the reasons for his senseless death. Why? Why? Why did this happen? I had prayed for this baby. How could his life be taken away when I was praying so hard? The pain was unbearable and I kept apologizing to my child: "Baby, I am sorry I failed you. Please forgive me."

I chanted to make sense of the situation, and my Buddhist friends became my strength once again. They helped me appreciate that the truth had been revealed before Adil came into this world. He would have suffered greatly if he had been born, and so would the rest of our family. This was the protection invoked by my sincere prayers. I was so lost in my pain that this had not struck me.

The next day when I arrived home from the hospital, I went straight to my Buddhist altar. I kneeled down, wanting to chant, but I was unable to speak the words. I chanted in my mind until the prayers within became the words on my lips. I apologized from the depths of my life for whatever I had done that had resulted in the death of my child. His loss was clearly the result of our combined karmas.

In that moment, I understood the law of cause and effect that I had learned in my Buddhist study. I had created causes in my life that had attracted the death of my child. But my child had also created causes that had resulted in him having Down syndrome. Our combined karmas had brought us together and had resulted in tremendous pain. The fact he did not come into this world to suffer more was also karma—good karma.

On May 3, 2001, I offered to share my experience at a special Buddhist meeting. As I began to speak, tears came to the eyes of the women in the group. Many of them approached me afterward and spoke with me, offering sincere words of empathy and sharing their own experiences. Through these heart-to-heart conversations, I began to heal, and I felt the energy returning to move on with my life. I had let go of my pain by sharing it with my fellow members. Now the words of Dr. Ikeda in one of the books I had studied made complete sense to me: "Buddhism gives value and meaning to everything in life—every past suffering and all present trials."

My faith deepened greatly due to this experience, as did my courage. I found myself naturally turning to my Buddhist practice for an answer to every situation.

In September of the same year, I had the opportunity to visit an orphanage and make a financial contribution on behalf of a foreign guest who was staying at the hotel where I worked. I sought official permission to visit the orphanage and deliver food I had bought for the children. The orphanage was about eighteen and a half miles away from my place of work. I arrived there with all the goodies and visited with the kids for a bit, hugging and speaking with them. I could see they were craving love so badly, and I was choked with emotion.

Just as I was leaving, the nun in charge, Sister Andrea, invited me to visit the baby room, saying three adorable new babies had recently arrived at the orphanage. I walked into the baby room and was introduced to the sleeping infants. One of them, a tiny girl named Leela (the youngest of the three at ten days old), drew me more than the other two for some reason. She was the cutest thing I had ever seen, and as I held her I felt an intense surge of emotion. She brought to mind my Adil; he would have been born that month if I had not had to let him go. Where was he now, I wondered? Dragging myself back to the present, I refocused on the baby in my arms. I cooed to her in baby language and played with her for almost half an hour, though she was half asleep. I had to force myself to walk out the door and return to work.

That night and over the next couple of weeks, I prayed for Leela. I could not seem to help myself. She was constantly in my thoughts. I spoke with Sister Andrea about adopting her, but she very firmly told me that Leela was going to be given to another family. This family had already adopted a baby boy from the orphanage, and Sister Andrea wanted Leela to be part of their family. Besides, she said, I already had my own child, and the orphanage had a very long waiting list of parents without children.

Despite Sister Andrea's words, I took Jag and Aman to meet Leela. I had not given up hope even though I had no reason to think we had a chance. I decided to stop stressing about it. I got busy over the next few weeks with a Buddhist meeting, but I continued to stay in touch with the orphanage about Leela. On November 30, in my routine follow-up call, I was informed that Leela had a blood infection and was in the hospital. I was terribly afraid for her and wanted desperately to see her with my own eyes.

That evening at the final preparations for the general meeting, I was very disturbed. The only thing I could focus on was praying for Leela and her protection. I had a strange karmic bond with this child, one that did not let me sleep at night due to my concern for her.

Our meeting the next morning was a grand success. Right after the event, I went along with my friend Nilesh to see Leela in the hospital. We picked up Sister Andrea from the orphanage along the way. To my surprise, the nurse at the hospital started to accuse me of abandoning little Leela the moment she saw me. Because she saw a resemblance in our faces, she thought Leela was my daughter and that I was the wicked mother who had abandoned this precious girl. I was taken aback at her vehemence. Thankfully, Sister Andrea corrected her, and I was escorted by the now-embarrassed nurse to see the baby.

Leela was a premature and underweight infant. The infection made her look even more fragile, and I could see her veins through her skin. Several needles were poking into her small body, and seeing her there, lying helpless, made my tears flow.

For the first time, I saw Leela with her eyes fully open and awake. I felt that same strange and deep heart-to-heart connection with her. Was it my imagination or were her eyes trying to tell me something?

I decided to take the risk of asking Sister Andrea if I could take Leela home. There were more than twenty-five babies in the care of one nun in the baby room at the orphanage, and there was no way she could manage such a sick child. Unexpectedly, Sister Andrea accepted my offer. She asked me to call back within two days once Leela had been released from the hospital. This was a complete turnabout! I was thrilled, but now had another bridge to cross—getting Jag on the same page. I practiced my speech to him all the way home in the car. My next surprise came when Jag put up no resistance whatsoever. All he said was, "She can stay with us, but for no more than two days, Pooja."

I concealed my joy at the victory.

The next morning, I woke with a high fever and a sore throat. I had no energy to move and could only chant in my mind. I prayed to be in good health the next day to bring Leela home, but instead I felt even sicker. I made the decision to bring Leela home anyway. I did not want to risk Sister Andrea and Jag changing their minds. Jag and I drove to the orphanage and Leela, dressed up in new clothes, was handed over to us along with her favorite milk bottle.

This was a big triumph. In India, orphanages are very strict, especially with the adoption of a female child. History has taught them that female children are often abused, and they are very cautious as a result. Rightly so!

When we reached home, I dug out all of Aman's baby clothes that I had saved for my second baby. I changed Leela and nicely powdered her to tempt Aman into carrying her—but he completely ignored her. He wanted a baby brother and not a baby sister. Since I had a severe viral infection, I had to stay away from Leela as she had just come out of hospital and her resistance was really low. She slept next to Jag in our bedroom while I used the guest room.

Leela cried most of the night, a symptom of her not yet being fully recovered, not to mention the fact that she was in a strange environment with strange people. Jag stayed awake with her and carried her around all night, trying to make her feel secure and calm her down so she could sleep. I could hear his voice as he talked to her. The next morning when

I peeked into our bedroom, Leela's tiny hand was wrapped around Jag's finger and both of them were blissfully asleep.

I stayed out of Leela's way both nights. When Jag was away at work, I looked after her with the help of the maids at home. Exactly forty-eight hours after bringing Leela home, as promised to Jag, I offered to take her back. To my surprise, Jag refused. He wanted to adopt her. Mission accomplished! I danced for joy.

We still had to take Leela back to the orphanage and convince Sister Andrea of our plan, as well as do the paperwork. I knew it could easily take six months before the process could be completed. A friend of mine had adopted a baby girl and it had taken almost a year before she and her husband were allowed to bring their baby home.

I was saddened at the thought of leaving Leela back at the orphanage again, but short of kidnapping her and disappearing somewhere, I had no choice. I held her in my arms all the way to the orphanage and chanted in my heart. We reached the orphanage far too soon for my liking. As we settled down in Sister Andrea's office, I was about to plead to adopt the child again when the nun pulled the carpet from under my feet by handing over her lawyer's card. She suggested we go meet the lawyer right away and start the adoption process.

I looked at her in disbelief, and was even more astonished when she said we could take Leela home with us right away.

It was unbelievable; my sincere prayer had proven more powerful than the strict adoption laws of the country! I quickly dragged Jag out of the orphanage with Leela before Sister Andrea could say another word, promising to bring Leela back for a visit very soon.

And so Leela became our daughter, Reyna—the gorgeous Reyna, fun-loving and full of life. It took six months and a few hundred dollars in lawyers' fees before she was officially ours in May 2002. Reyna is eight years old now, and I feel Jag and I are only conduits for this beautiful child to fulfill her mission in this world.

The girl I brought home for two days became my cherished daughter and the apple of her father's eye. For all his resistance, Jag is completely wrapped around Reyna's little finger. Aman soon got over his desire for a little brother and taught Reyna to play with cars instead of dolls. And Reyna was unconditionally accepted by both Jag's and my families as their newest member.

I will never fully understand why we had to lose Adil, but I do know that my biggest sorrow became the cause of my greatest joy in the space of seven months. The loss of Adil and arrival of Reyna were also the reason for Jag's strengthened connection to Buddhism. Until Reyna came into our lives, Jag's practice lacked conviction. He chanted and attended meetings, but it seemed to me he was not experiencing the same joy I was from chanting *Nam-myoho-renge-kyo*. He seemed to be testing the waters of the vast ocean of Nichiren Buddhism, vacillating between excitement about the philosophy and a tentative involvement. Reyna was his turning point. After we brought her home, Jag often held Reyna in his lap as he prayed; the room would vibrate with the energy he exuded, and baby Reyna would stare at him without blinking, captivated by her father.

Adil would have been born in September 2001, and Reyna was born on September 19, 2001. Reyna, Adil, and I are connected in a way that goes beyond the realm of this life. Buddhism believes that life is eternal and we are reborn again and again. I felt the truth of that throbbing in every part of my being. To date, I still pray for my Adil and his happiness. I am thankful I suffered so he did not have to. He washed away negative karma by coming to me and then leaving to be reborn so he could live a life of good health and happiness. Wherever he is, I know he is protected and enjoying life among loved ones. My daily prayers for him are ensuring that.

As much as everyone tells me that Reyna is fortunate, I believe we are as, if not more, fortunate to have met her. She has brought immense joy to our lives, and our combined karmas have created much good fortune for our family. I feel blessed to be her mother, and not a day passes when I do not offer appreciation for her presence in my life.

When Reyna grew a little older, I became stressed about the best possible way to let her know she is the child of my heart but not the child of my body. I feared sharing this knowledge with her, concerned about the impact it might have on her feelings for us and for herself. It was my insecurity and lack of confidence at being able to communicate how much she meant to me that got in my way. What if she asked about her parents and wanted to meet them? What if she doubted my love for her? There were so many "what ifs" swirling around in my mind that I felt overwhelmed. Only prayer helped me overcome this hesitation. As I prayed, I felt emotionally stronger and more secure. My confidence rose and completely changed my outlook. From within came the response that nothing can change the depth of my love for my child—not even Reyna herself. If my love for her was true, and I knew it was, Reyna would love me as her mother for the rest of her life.

Reyna had every right to know about her birth parents and her start in life when the time came. I had to keep the lines of communication open at all times, and love and nurture her unconditionally. I chanted for wisdom and sought guidance from my Buddhist leaders about the best way to share the truth with her. I wanted her to learn about what happened from us, and not hear about it by accident.

Jag and I were able to speak with Reyna about this in September 2008. Jag brought some books home from the library that helped us do this in the form of a story. So far, Reyna seems unaffected about the truth of her origins. When she grows up and starts to ask questions, I hope this portion of the book will communicate to her how much she means to us all.

Treasures of My Heart

Nothing is more precious to me than my children. I want them to grow up to be wonderful human beings. It is a challenge to guide them—more so nowadays when children have such huge exposure to the outside world. My parents did not have to compete with computer games and PlayStations to get my sister and me to do our homework. There were no soap operas teaching us how to ask a boy out on a date. I am sure my mother is glad that I did not have a Hannah Montana to worship and imitate.

I have struggled with Aman and his education considerably. He started school in India at the age of three. The Indian education system is overwhelmingly focused on academic performance, and there is hardly any time for play and fun. Aman would go to school at 7:45 a.m., come back home exhausted at 4 p.m., and after a quick lunch in front of the TV, watching like a zombie, he was rushed by our driver to his tutor and brought back home at 6:45, after which he had a fifteen-minute window to play with his friends. He had to come home by 7 p.m. to do his homework and have a quick dinner before going to bed.

We did not know any other life, and we initially had no clue what this hectic schedule was doing to our precious child. Aman was an angry little boy from the moment he came into the world, and this schooling regime made him even angrier. He was constantly being rushed here and there. The academic pressure was too much for him, and I was forever stressed because his teachers made it clear they were unhappy with his academic performance.

There were sixty students in Aman's class, and the teacher had no time to pay individual attention to him or give him the extra time he needed. In the Indian education system, Aman was like a square peg in a round hole. I was frustrated because I could not understand what was truly going wrong or determine the solution required. All I knew was that Aman was attending one of the most prestigious schools, and that my friends would give anything to enrol their children there. I realized later that I was trying to force Aman to fit into a rigid mold, which only resulted in more anger and rebellion from him. His teachers started to label him as a "not very bright" child who "misbehaved." Aman responded to every one of these labels by becoming naughty and disengaging from schoolwork.

I sought spiritual guidance many times about Aman and my concerns with his behavior. One piece of advice I received from a spiritual mentor struck a chord with me, and I still follow her words today. She said, "When we pray for our children, we pray for all the problems that confront us, like sickness, education, etc. But it is important to pray for their happiness, and for them to grow consistently and contribute to creating a peaceful world as capable leaders. Such prayers are all encompassing." So true!

It dawned on me that we needed to help Aman find joy and passion so that he looked forward to each day. It was not easy to find something to motivate him to enjoy school; his love of sports was not finding a ready outlet there. We needed to give Aman more options than he had, but we lacked clarity on how best to do that in the Indian system where everyone was expected to attend a prestigious school, study hard, and excel at academics. And so, Aman and Reyna became the deciding factor in our move to Canada. Jag had a dream for them; he knew they would have opportunities in Canada that were better suited to their interests. I did not see it so clearly at the time, but I do now.

Aman is a different child since we moved to Canada. He loves school and I am seeing strengths I never knew he had. He plays sports and is a great help at home. He is also fantastic with little kids. He plays with them and genuinely likes them, and they seem to adore him as well. All of these qualities were recognized in the after-school program he attended in Vancouver. It was so rewarding to hear his supervisors praise him for his sense of responsibility and compassion. Because of the leadership qualities Aman displayed and his ability to be a mentor to smaller kids, his teachers appointed him as a leader and moved him out of the group of children his own age to one composed of children a year older than him. He became the youngest leader in that group.

I was filled with pride every time I heard the day care supervisors praise my son. All the pain and humiliation of being reprimanded about my child's poor behavior and lack of academic ability were forgotten. Aman was now in an environment that brought out the best in him and made his strengths shine. The recognition of his unique abilities made me realize how wrong I had been to try and push Aman into doing what was expected of him, instead of trying to understand what his life really needed.

Had I not been through this myself as a child? How had I allowed this to happen? These questions brought me deep regret, but beyond making a commitment to be wiser in the future, I had to let the regret go and focus instead on the here and now. I now know Aman will be fine. As long as I continue to make an effort to understand my child and guide him with love, he will grow into a fine human being.

If for no other reason, the opportunity for Aman was worth all the turmoil of moving to a new country and starting life all over again.

Being the Best I Can

As a woman, I have to balance a full-time job, a family, my personal aspirations and goals, my spiritual practice, and the everyday mundane chores of life. My Buddhist beliefs help me do all of the above joyfully and live a life of value-creation, in rhythm with the universe—but this is not always so easy.

Over the years there have been several times when I had to leave home in the evening to chant or attend a meeting. Leaving the kids to attend a Buddhist activity sometimes felt like an unwinnable tug-of-war within me. When Aman was little, I experienced such pangs of guilt that I sometimes took him to meetings with me, even though I knew he was quite a distraction there. He was a restless child, always grabbing things and investigating them. It disturbed the other members and that bothered me a lot. Members attended meetings to find peace and solace, and I did not want my child's antics to take that away from them. I sometimes lost patience with Aman and was tempted to walk out.

I sought guidance on this matter and was advised to pray that Aman support my spiritual journey and Buddhist practice. I followed this advice, and soon Aman started to quiet down and play on his own while I contributed to the proceedings. Later, we were able to afford a live-in maid to take care of him while I attended meetings. Today, Aman babysits his little sister when Jag and I both have an evening commitment. He does an awesome job, and takes the responsibility of caring for Reyna very seriously.

Although my dedication to my family and my desire for spiritual growth are sometimes challenging to uphold at once, time has taught me that my family receives great protection through my contribution to Buddhism. Interacting with other mothers practicing the philosophy and learning from their experiences has helped me be a better parent.

Early on when my children were very young, I would come home from work to a mess of toys and dishes lying around the living area. The sight made me livid. Without asking my family how they were or what kind of day they had, I criticized them for making a mess, running around the room cleaning up and shouting at them.

I realized the error of my ways when a close friend shared pearls of wisdom about how our attitude affects whether our children have the opportunity to take up this powerful philosophy. If we come home from Buddhist meetings in a state of anger, she said, our children will connect that state of mind with the Buddhist philosophy. The thought that will cross their minds is, "Gosh! If this is what happens to my mom when she attends a Buddhist meeting, I definitely want no part of it."

I went home that night thinking that if I wanted to lead my children to Buddhism, I could not allow them to feel negative about it—and they would feel negative if they perceived it as being my priority instead of them. They would come to resent it, and this was true of my career and other interests as well.

Even though I accepted all of this intellectually, it took me a long time to change my attitude. I would react instinctively, and then in the evening when I was sitting in front of my altar to chant, I would reflect on my day. I would go over all that had happened, thinking of situations I could have handled better. I would resolve once again to shower my children with love when I came home, and close my eyes to the cleanliness of the house.

I have turned to prayer to communicate better with my children in other ways as well. Even when I am patient, my words do not always get through to my children. When I say, "Please be safe, honey!" I realize it has zero impact on them. Therefore, every morning when I do my chanting, I shower both my kids with prayers before they step out of the house. I focus on connecting to them deeply so the channels of communication are always open between us.

The mornings are my favorite time of day now. This is *my* time, when

I can communicate with the vast universe, undisturbed for at least an hour. Before the madness of the morning takes over, I empower myself with prayer. It took a lot of discipline and self-training to commence my day at my altar—but so did going to the gym to lose weight! It was tempting to get other tasks out of the way before sitting to chant, but when I left it to the very end of the morning to-do list, it was rushed and I became stressed about getting to work on time.

I decided to change the order of my morning activities when I attended a training program at my workplace. The session helped me understand that I needed to prioritize and do things that were important to me first, instead of always leaving my needs for the last. The facilitator spoke about living true to oneself, about being consistent with one's values. My spiritual growth is high on my list of priorities. Once I realized that, I was drawn like a magnet to my altar in the mornings.

The very first silent payer I now do in the mornings is to ask for protection. I close my eyes for a brief moment and invite every Buddhist God in the universe to join me. At this point I pray for no accidents, for good health, and for the protection of my children from negative forces within and without. I ask for wisdom and patience with my children, because I need both in abundance. I am very selective about what to reprimand them about and what I will not allow them to get away with. I want to build their characters and help them be compassionate persons of integrity. Of course it's important they keep their rooms clean, but I know that if I start to point out everything, my words will be ignored. Then when something is really important, it will receive the same response and lack of attention. So I pick and choose carefully what I want to discuss with them, and how I say it. I may let petty things go, but I keep a very close watch on anything character-building like honesty, integrity, and sharing with others.

It takes a lot of effort to say no to my children, and there are days when I want to give up and let them do what they want, even if it is not right. I seek ways and means to stay positive and happy throughout the day to ensure I have unflagging energy and freshness even in the evening, because that is the only time I get to spend with my kids. No matter what time it is, I cannot afford to let fatigue overwhelm me, nor can I succumb to lethargy and be too tired to show my kids the right way. This, like everything else in my life, is an ongoing process. I fail sometimes and at other times I succeed, but my true victory lies in making a continuous effort.

When I get such flashes of wisdom, how I wish I had encountered this life-transforming philosophy at Reyna's age. This thought makes me want to guide my children to Buddhism while they are still young. I often share Buddhist experiences with Aman; in fact, whenever Jag or I come across an encouraging story about extraordinary human achievement, we make it a point to share it with our son. I also buy simple Buddhist storybooks for Reyna, and have been reading them to her since she was three. Additionally, Jag and I encourage both our children to pray. I would be delighted if they did this regularly on their own, but for now, even thirty seconds of prayer before they leave home in the morning and before they go to bed is sufficient. I know they believe in praying only because I believe in it. They are young and they listen to me, so if I tell them to chant, they do. But I want them to come to faith on their own accord, since self-motivated faith is the best kind. They deserve the same freedom to make their own choices that I was given by my parents.

I feel like a master juggler at times, trying to do justice to all my roles as a mother, a wife, an employee, and an active member of my community. Time is precious and limited, and I have so many aspirations for my children, my other loved ones, and my own life. I have learned to prioritize. Every day I ration my time carefully and distribute it based on my life's priorities. I cannot forsake my spiritual growth to take care of my kids, and do not want to sacrifice my personal dreams to make money for survival.

I want it all.

I practice Buddhism precisely to achieve all the things in my life that are important to me, and very often in the bargain receive a number of things that are less important as well. Practicing Buddhism does not mean I am able to get my way all the time. The beauty of it is the joy it helps me find in life when things are going well and also when things are all awry. That is enlightenment, in my understanding. Life has its way of throwing us off guard all the time. We need a strong foundation and support system that will stand the test of time and absorb all the curve balls that life is constantly throwing our way, and each of us has to find our own unique source to build that for ourselves and our families.

I am determined to be happy no matter what. No longer do I believe that I am a victim of my circumstances or other people's actions. By no means is it easy; I fail frequently. But when I do, I gather myself to start all over again, pulling from deep within me the strength and determination to begin anew.

Vancouver, Here I Come

February 2006 was another new beginning, another opportunity to start life afresh, this time in a new country with new friends.

As mentioned earlier, our kids were the greatest motivation for Jag and me to apply for permanent residency in Canada. I didn't really want to leave India, but Jag had his heart set on it and I wanted him to be able to fulfill his dream. He had a high-pressure job that made him miserable with constant travel and intense physical and mental demands, and he simply needed a fresh start. He was also convinced that the change would be very good for Aman. Canada's school system, he said, would give our son opportunities to get involved in a number of sports and arts-related options. After several months of thought, I agreed to start the immigration process. Despite my internal misgivings, I wanted nothing more than for my family to be happy.

We applied for immigration to Canada in June 2001, and the application had just been processed when the September 11 attacks occurred. As a result, a process that should have taken less than thirty-six months took sixty months instead.

So much changed in our lives from the time we made the application to the time our visas were stamped, allowing us entry into Canada. We adopted Reyna legally. We bought our own home and our first car. I changed jobs and my career took off. And one of the best things to happen to me was a trip to Japan to attend a Buddhist conference.

At the event I met many other practitioners, most importantly a senior Buddhist leader from Canada, Tony Meers, who helped me overcome my concerns about immigrating. By good fortune I sat next to Tony on the bus on the way back from a meeting. On learning he was from Canada, I shared with him our immigration plans. Jag and I had been going back and forth for several months about the move, me completely against it and he absolutely for it. I was fearful of being isolated in a strange new country, especially at a time when my career was doing so well in India; I saw no point in going to another country and having to prove myself with a new employer after fifteen years of a consistently progressive and successful career in Chennai.

I poured my heart out to Tony. He listened patiently, then told me about several members from India who now lived in Toronto. He had seen their struggles, and said that moving was ultimately a decision I had to make. I was hoping he would say something that would enable me to know what I should do, which, of course, he did not. Giving guidance does not mean we tell people what to do or what not to do; it means helping them find their own way. It means listening to them wholeheartedly and drawing forth the wisdom they have within. That is exactly what Tony did for me.

Our immigration process had been stalled for three years, but suddenly, after my trip to Japan, things started to move at high speed. Exactly twelve months later, we had visas in our hands with an injunction to be in Canada by February 14, 2006. I did not want to leave India, but when the visas came through I took the view that there was a reason we had been approved and that we were meant to be in Canada. Jag and I discussed the situation at length before finally deciding to make the move. We told ourselves that, if nothing else, we could look at it as a very expensive vacation, and definitely the biggest adventure of our lives to date.

We had gone through the entire process with the help of a consultant. As part of our contract, the consultant was supposed to assist in the settlement process, including providing job assistance once we reached Canada. However, the contract stipulated that we had to settle in Toronto, so we booked our tickets for this city and sourced a few contacts there.

A month prior to our departure, my cousin Poonam and her husband, Manu, who lived in Seattle, convinced us to move to Vancouver instead of Toronto, primarily because of the weather and their proximity to the west coast city. Since they were close family who had our best interests at heart, we took their advice very seriously and chanted about it. I was uncertain what the best choice was for us. If we moved to Vancouver, all the money we had paid to the consultant would be wasted, as they would offer no assistance outside of Toronto. How would we find work and a place to stay? We knew no one in Vancouver. Nevertheless, we decided on the west coast location.

Poonam and Manu became our protective forces during the entire moving process. They came to the airport to pick us up, all the way from Seattle, and helped us find accommodation. They gave us helpful advice on every aspect of North American living, from the most economical grocery shopping options to career opportunities. Poonam and I are almost the same age, and we had gone through all the ups and downs of childhood and the tortuous teenage years together in Mumbai. Although we had not been in regular contact since she had married thirteen years earlier and moved to the U.S., and she had no obligation to do so much for me or my family, she was simply wonderful.

In the weeks following our arrival in Vancouver, Poonam and Manu visited us several weekends in a row, staying in hotels and showing us around our new city so we could appreciate its beauty and start finding our way around. I don't know if my words can do justice to the beauty of Vancouver. The fresh air, the purity of the water, the clear blue skies, and the snow-capped mountains all made me feel like I was in heaven. The peace and quiet and the wonderful people I met on the streets of this gorgeous city made me want to bow my head in humility. The tree-lined street outside our home, with gorgeous red and golden flowers that were just beginning to bloom, heralded spring and lifted my heart, which had been heavy since leaving my homeland and loved ones there. When we drove over the Lion's Gate Bridge to West Vancouver, crossing a vast waterway heading out to the ocean, I felt like I could reach out and grab the stars, the sky seemed so close. That drive made me feel like an angel sitting on her own personal cloud instead of a mortal sitting in a car.

While we were thrilled by the scenic beauty of Vancouver in our first few days there, we were also aware that starting a whole new life in a new city and country would have its trials and tribulations. The first night I wept and told Jag, "We have made a mistake! I want to go back." I did this several times over the next year.

Our rented home was a tiny one-room studio apartment with a wee little kitchen, and we had paid in advance for two months. It came fully furnished and cost us an obscene amount of money. It is unbelievable to me now that we arrived in Canada with only $7,000 in our hands. I shake my head in disbelief. How on earth did we think that was enough? Wanting to hold on to our property in India, we had rented it out completely furnished to a friend, so along with sustaining ourselves in Canada we also had to take care of our mortgage and other financial commitments in India.

I look back at our departure from India and am amazed at the courage we had to take the actions we did. That courage came from a complete lack of awareness of what we were facing, which was good. Had I known what lay in store for us I would have refused to make the move. I would still be living within my comfort zone in India, with my same old ways, and would have missed out on all the learning and growth I have had.

We definitely had no choice but to find work immediately. I was insecure and terrified, but I tried to rise above it. I started applying for jobs right away, and attended my first interview within a week of landing in Vancouver. I had created a "Vancouver goal card," and first on my list was to find a management position.

Many well-meaning people I met warned me, "Just take whatever you get. Minimum wage is great. And make sure you apply to all the grocery stores; they are always looking for cashiers. Jag should apply as a security guard; he will get paid more with them, especially if he works graveyards." It was depressing to hear stories about highly educated professionals from my country giving up on their careers in Canada and taking any job they could find to survive. I refused to accept this as a reality for my and Jag's lives.

At one point, Jag seriously contemplated applying with a security company because of the advice he was receiving, but I stubbornly dug in my heels. Sitting on a park bench one evening while Aman and Reyna played, Jag and I were enjoying some spring sunshine but feeling dismal about our future. "No way!" I said. "We have not traveled halfway across the world to allow our dreams to come crashing down around us. I will take the next flight back if you do that." He had been a national sales manager with one of India's biggest facilities management companies. I was willing to accept that he might not get such a senior position in Vancouver, but surely he could get something in his field of expertise.

I vowed to do everything possible to make that happen. I prayed like never before to challenge the situation. It took all my inner strength, courage, and persistence to keep my dream alive. One step at a time, slowly but surely, I had to find a way to make our hopes a reality.

During the first two months in Vancouver, I frequently picked up my goal card and read it over and over. Reviewing my objectives morning and evening helped me refresh my determination and stay on track without compromising. At times, it was tempting to give in and accept whatever job came my way. I had to wage an internal war not to settle for anything but the absolute best.

While I went on interviews and walked into organizations to drop off my résumé, Jag was yet to commence looking for work wholeheartedly. Instead, he stayed at home with Reyna. She was then four and a half years old, too young to start school. Aman, however, got into a very good school. The only problem was the distance from our place. We had landed in Vancouver during the coldest part of the year, and it rained all day. The temperature in Chennai never dropped below 80 degrees Fahrenheit, and during the summer it rose to over 100 degrees, so the Vancouver cold was unbearable for all four of us. We could not yet afford a car, nor did Jag or I have a B.C. driver's license, so we had to walk Aman to and from school with little Reyna tagging along. Jag did this most often as I was busy with interviews. He usually ended up carrying Reyna because she was so cold and tired.

I attended at least twenty-five interviews over three weeks before I received my first job offer at $12 an hour as a client relations executive with a company in downtown Vancouver. I was to start work on March 1; however, Jag was still unable to look for a job as we could not leave Reyna and Aman alone. We searched for a preschool/day care for Reyna and an after-school program for Aman. A center offering both programs was located right next door to our home, but it had a long waiting list, as did other similar schools in the area. We felt helpless and stuck. We needed money to survive, which meant we both had to find jobs, but if we could not find help with the kids, one of us had to stay behind, which would delay our job searches and the process of getting settled. The alternative was for Jag and me to work at different times during the day so one of us was always available for the kids—but that meant sacrificing our time together as a family, and we needed each other now more than ever.

We were faced with a series of unhappy choices. It seemed like we would have to compromise and let go of our family time. We both wanted to have dinner together with the kids every evening and listen to their new experiences, but we were at a loss as to how we could make ends meet financially and still be together for the evening meal. I remember one discouraging evening when I made twenty calls to all the after-school programs in the area and received no positive responses.

The situation was so frustrating, and I felt very angry that we had been left in the dark about so many important aspects about life in Vancouver. If we had known that child care was such a challenge and so expensive, we would have done things differently. Jag and I were the only support our children had in this country, and sensing our fear and insecurity must have been worrisome for them. Nothing mattered more than their happiness and security, but we were unsure how we could provide that with our scarce financial resources if both of us could not work. Not being able to provide adequately for our children was a terrible feeling.

Not knowing how to overcome this situation, I sat down and prayed for a way out. The next day, on his way back from taking Aman to school, Jag dropped by the preschool closest to our home and managed to speak to the lady who headed the center. She became another protective force. She gave Reyna an immediate spot in the preschool and agreed to take Aman into the after-school program. She was moved by our situation and went out of her way to assist us. I had spoken to this school and day care twice already, and their response had been negative both times. So how did this situation change overnight? The answer was very clear to me: earnest prayers can move mountains.

The day I started work was the day both Aman and Reyna started their programs with this facility. Only later would we become aware that this was one of the most sought-after preschool and after-school centers in the whole city.

This development gave Jag the much-needed opportunity to start making his applications and find a job. Unlike me, Jag got a positive response to the very first interview he attended, and he landed the job. He joined a company as a call center executive at $12 an hour. He managed to land this position within the industry he knew well from his job in India: facilities management. Despite the fact that both of us now had decent jobs, we were very clear with each other that we would continue to look for management positions more suited to our skills and experience.

The organization I joined was not very well-managed or professionally run. It was a fairly young company that lacked expertise. It was also a completely new industry for me—internet gambling. I was very confused, and received no training nor input. In fact, for the first two weeks, I was given only a chair to sit on, with no desk or computer to call my own. I had to sit at the desk of another young lady who was half my age, forced to listen to her calling her boyfriend every two hours. There was not enough work to do and she and a man hired a few days before me spent half their time on the internet and the other half chatting with each other. It was a very strange situation to be in, and I disliked it intensely. I was used to a high-stress, demanding job, and this inactivity drove me crazy. By the time I reached home each day, I was depressed and dejected. After two weeks I was finally given my own office space. This should have made me happy, but I still had nothing to do. So, just like my colleagues, I started surfing the net to try and stay occupied.

After forty-five days of this, I landed another job as a sales coordinator in the hotel industry at almost double the pay. I was offered the position despite the fact that the owners of the hotel were not in favor of hiring me because I did not have "Canadian experience." This was a line I heard over and over again at several interviews I attended. I was either overqualified for the position or I did not have "Canadian experience." Either way, I was rejected. Several times I was told that I had an impressive background, but what was the point? My impressive background did not give me the break I needed into the Canadian job market. As predicted by my well-wishers, I was being rejected and pushed into settling for a job just so I could survive. But I was not every immigrant. I fought the system through the power of my prayer.

The general manager of this three-star property became another protective force. He was a great supporter and invested over two weeks to train and empower me so I could be successful. I started to generate revenues for the hotel within the first month of being there. The owners were very pleased with my performance and initiated direct interaction with me. However, within a few weeks, I noticed undercurrents of jealousy and resentment flowing among the other employees. No professional was willing to waste their time in such a workplace, and someone resigned almost every other day because of the negative energy. I allowed myself to be influenced by all the grapevine gossip, and in a few days had worked myself into such a frenzy that I was desperate to get out of there as well. My contract required me to give a month's notice if I completed the three-month probation, and I did not want to stay around that long. Financially, however, I could not afford to quit without another job to go to.

I could not sleep because of all the stress I was feeling, and would some days wake up at 3 a.m. and start chanting so I could find the courage to go to work. A friend had gifted me a placard bearing the following words from Dr. Ikeda's book, *Faith into Action*, and I read it over and over again to keep myself strong:

> When your determination changes, everything will begin to move in the direction you desire. The moment you resolve to be victorious, every nerve and fibre in your being will immediately orient itself toward your success. On the other hand, if you think, "This is never going to work out," then at that instant every cell in your being will be defeated and give up the fight. Then everything really will move in the direction of failure.

Meanwhile, Jag was doing well with his company. His potential had been recognized, and the owners of his firm rewarded him with small bonuses on almost every paycheck. His company was a start-up, and Jag had the experience to take it to great heights. This was recognized by the owners, but they didn't offer him the promotion or the salary he deserved until he tendered his resignation.

Within two and a half months of joining his original firm, Jag was picked up by a much larger organization in the same business with a substantial increase in salary. The first company woke up to reality and tried every strategy to retain him, including offering him big bucks and the position of general manager. But it was too late; he had given his word to the new company and had accepted their signing bonus. This was a great benefit for us, and the financial advantages did not end there. Having heard about my professional background, Jag's former employer asked to meet with me. He wanted to assess my suitability for a senior management position. This was great news, and yet another protective force emerged. My 3 a.m. chanting sessions were clearly bearing fruit.

I met Jag's former boss for an interview and was offered the senior management position with a higher salary, all within one day. I gladly quit my job with the hotel just one day before my probation period ended, and started work with this new organization.

I feel deep gratitude to the first two organizations that employed me and the people there who gave me an opportunity. Were it not for them, our financial survival would have been impossible. And had I been comfortable and enjoyed myself with them, I never would have pushed myself to search for new opportunities. I would not have tried to reach for the light of the sun, and instead would have settled for the light from the stars.

Uprooting Deep-rooted Karma

My career in Vancouver progressed reasonably well over the first two years of immigrating to Canada. I changed jobs three times, but eventually settled down with a good organization. However, one major obstacle to total career satisfaction was what I called my "boss" karma.

I have always been quite a career-minded and ambitious woman. I have been working since the age of nineteen, and have been financially independent since twenty-five. The challenge of a professional career gives me a certain high. However, I have continually struggled with my bosses at work. It often seemed like they were finding fault with me no matter how hard I worked, and I had to go to great lengths to win them over. As a result, one of my constant prayers over the past ten years has been to get along with the people I report to.

My troubles with this were at their peak when I started practicing Buddhism back in Chennai. I just could not get along with Anil, the manager I reported to at the hotel. I seemed to bring out the worst in him. He often put me down in front of my team members, and constantly found fault with me. I thought I was hardworking and sincere, and my clients loved me, but this man could see no good in me. I disliked working with him as much as he seemed to dislike working with me. It came to a point where I desperately wanted to quit my job but could not afford to financially. I searched for new employment, but couldn't find anything suitable. It went on like this for four years. I suffered terribly and often felt frustrated at my helplessness, but I could not seem to change the situation at my workplace.

I sought guidance from my spiritual mentors, who told me to chant for the happiness of my boss. I needed to send him positive energy vibes. That sounded absolutely impossible! It was an effort not to wish ill on him, so chanting for his happiness was something I did not think I would be able to do. Reluctantly, I decided to follow my leaders' guidance, initially chanting the words without meaning them. I prayed for Anil's happiness but was hoping inside that he would be unhappy and pay the price for all the torment he was putting me through.

As I continued to chant for him, however, I made a mental shift without realizing it. I actually started to wish him genuine happiness. The moment I changed the anger and dislike in my heart to compassion, Anil could no longer affect me negatively. It was no longer easy for him to provoke me.

About the same time I conquered my challenges with Anil, a new job opportunity arose with an international organization. I was thrilled to put my old job and boss behind me. Anil had completely changed toward me by then; he actually pleaded with me to stay, but it was too late. I had already moved on in my head and my body was just waiting to follow. I excitedly looked forward to my new job and a new boss. But my joy was short-lived. I had taken my boss karma with me.

The new organization did not acknowledge my experience, and at one point it was almost like I was reporting to a fresh graduate. I had over ten years of working experience, so this was beyond my comprehension. Once again, I did not enjoy a great relationship with my manager, Vikas. There were good days and bad days. Clearly I still needed to expiate my negative karma, and it was no point trying to run away again.

I once had such a terrible argument with Vikas that I walked off the job. The human resources manager intervened and convinced me to come back, but I went through many struggles with that organization for more than two years. Eventually I managed to stabilize the situation and create a good reputation for myself, but I was demoted in 2004 when the management changed.

That was the year I had the opportunity to attend a Buddhist conference in Japan. When I spoke with a leader about the situation, I was guided to apologize for all the negative causes I had made, which were the reasons for this repetitive boss karma. I did that with all the sincerity I could muster. Because my pain was unbearable, the apology came from the very depth of my life. When I returned to India, I discovered that the old management team at my company had been reinstated. My old job profile and title were given back to me and my dignity was restored. My joy knew no bounds that day.

My career was at a high point when Jag and I decided to move to Canada, but once in my new country I received no recognition of my experience and worked in poorly managed companies for over a year. After changing jobs three times, I finally got the opportunity to work at a good company with fantastic senior management.

However, for the first time, I had a client that disliked me and wanted me out of my job. This time it was not my boss, but my client whom I dreaded speaking with. He was quite the terror, and my professional self-esteem dipped very low once again. History repeated itself because the money and the position were too good for me to walk away from.

I started praying for my client's happiness, determined to change this vicious cycle once and for all. It had gone on too long. I had to uproot the negative karma from the depth of my life, and as I chanted I knew the breakthrough would come.

Within four months, the client, Kevin, quit his job and a new person replaced him. My circle of friends in the client's organization expanded and I received so much recognition, I was touched. My new client requested that I be given responsibility for a larger area. Within six months of starting at my new firm, I had turned around the situation completely.

But that is not all. My deep boss karma was finally expiated. I now work with a wonderful team of senior managers who are so supportive of me, I am humbled. I have never been treated with as much respect and appreciation as I am now. I have all the independence I need to do my job. I look at my current manager, Steve, and feel like I have struck gold.

In return, I am ensuring that I do my best at work. Every day I offer gratitude for being able to change my job karma at last. I had been underpaid and often unappreciated for years. Every time things got better and I thought I had resolved the situation, I found the opposite to be true. This seesaw continued for nine years, and I never thought I would say this, but it was worth it. I came out of the situation stronger, more professional, and wiser. My current boss is teaching me new lessons on people management and human relations. I could not ask for more. I look forward to each day more than ever before.

Moving Ahead

After moving to Canada in 2006, I missed the craziness of my homeland. My constantly hectic schedule was not limited to my Buddhist activities; work had been extremely busy with intense pressure, as in many Asian countries. Although almost every management training program I attended included the topic of work-life balance, there was very little understanding of the concept in reality. I was always on call. Even at 10 p.m., I was alert to receiving a summons from work. My team members, my bosses, and my clients had unlimited access to my time. That is why we needed four people—two maids, a cook, and a driver—to help us manage our home.

India is noisy, filled with loud people, passionate spirit, a great go-get-it attitude, dinners at 10 p.m., working weekends, fun monthly dance parties at work, honking cars, and two-hour traffic jams. Everyone knows exactly what time which neighbor goes where; that is my home country. I missed this so much.

In Canada, the silence on the roads and the lack of people screaming from one desk to another unnerved me. I was used to the doorbell at home ringing no less than three times an hour, but in Vancouver I am surprised if it rings once a day. People dropped by our place in Chennai when they felt like it, whereas now I get invitations one month in advance. I often joked with Jag that back in India, none of us could sneeze without the next door neighbor knowing about it. In our new home, if someone died of a heart attack no one would know about it until the stink became unbearable.

In a way, my busy life back in India did not allow me enough time to slow down and spend time on introspection, nor did it allow me to focus on loved ones as much as I would have liked. I was always running around like a plucked chicken, with so much to do that the big stuff in my life always took a back seat. I got into the habit of dealing with the urgent and letting the important slide.

In North America, I decided to fill the often unbearable silence around me with the powerful sound of *Nam-myoho-renge-kyo*. Chanting abundantly has always created value in my life and filled any voids I might be feeling, and sure enough, once again my life opened in ways beyond my expectations.

When we moved to Vancouver, our first home was a small rented studio apartment with a little kitchen, as mentioned earlier. The four of us were cramped in the space. When I woke up early to chant, I had to whisper for fear of disturbing the rest of the family. I thought often about our lovely three-bedroom home in Chennai and my beautiful Buddhist altar there. The entirely new way of life we had to get accustomed to in Vancouver was overwhelming. Having to go downstairs to the basement to use the laundry room, shopping for groceries and having to carry heavy bags home, waiting for the bus in the cold weather—all of these things were like a nightmare of sorts. I had to learn to be resilient and self-reliant.

Every night when I was lying in bed, unable to sleep and staring at the ceiling, I focused my attention on appreciating the abundance of Vancouver. I reminded myself of the tortuous travel on the bus as a college student, and almost immediately my body would relax. I thought of all the hungry children I had seen every day as I traveled on the local trains back home, and I counted my new blessings. Vancouver is a land of plenty, beauty, and inexpressible joy. What on earth was I complaining about?

Undeniably, the scheduling and planning of household tasks was new to me. In India, I was used to a lot of help; if even one of our staff failed to show up for work, my life spun into a circus of sorts. Now forced to fend for myself, I realized it did not come naturally for me to do the laundry or make a grocery list. I was in a constant tizzy and always running out of supplies. When I went to Safeway, the only grocery store within walking distance of our home, the number of choices would bewilder me. Happily loading my grocery cart with packages that looked too attractive to resist, I wasted hundreds of dollars we could not afford. Everything required a new way of thinking that my upbringing had not prepared me for. It took several months before I got my bearings.

As we neared the end of our two-month contract with the studio apartment landlord, we started to walk around our neighborhood looking for "apartment available" signs. Because of our financial situation, we could afford only a one-bedroom place. However, no property manager was willing to rent a one-bedroom apartment to a family of four. They all asked for references, did not want children running around the apartment, and tried to convince us to rent a two-bedroom unit.

After repeated walks around our community, we finally met a property manager who took pity on us and was willing to sign a six-month contract. We were thrilled to finally have a place that would feel more like our home. We found a shopping cart outside our apartment one night, loaded it with all our bags, and moved our possessions in several trips back and forth. Poonam and Manu came from Seattle to help us move, bringing a U-Haul loaded with an entire bedroom set, a sofa set, and a television. Once again, they gave selflessly of their time, as well as their money, to help us settle in.

Our new home was at one of the busiest intersections in Vancouver. During the night I was often disturbed by screaming sirens, and Aman and Reyna had to sleep on a blanket on the living room floor. It wasn't ideal, but it was all we could afford. On the bright side, we had moved forward and that was what mattered. Jag and I had full-time jobs, the kids were settling into their school programs, and we had a place to call home, all in the space of two months. Each day brought a new challenge and a new learning opportunity along with it.

It is difficult for anyone to be positive every day, stay focused on their dreams, and live in the spirit of determination—at least it was difficult for me. I have tried different ways to move forward in my life—yoga, meditation, and so on. I have read self-help books by great authors such as Eckhart Tolle, Robin Sharma, and John Izzo. I have been nourished by the spirit of movies like *The Secret* and *The Pursuit of*

Happiness. Yet it was my grounding in Buddhist philosophy that helped me receive the wisdom of these inspirational teachers and their writings. Much of what they express echoes my belief in the possibility of creating a harmonious world by becoming peaceful individuals. How can we be at peace with one another if we are not at peace with ourselves?

Even after choosing my spiritual path, I was not always at peace with myself. I compartmentalized my life: compartment one was family, compartment two was my Buddhist practice, compartment three was my career. However, it is only in the last year that this complex jigsaw puzzle of life has come together for me. This is, by and large, the result of the support of the *sangha* (group) of believers and the positive outcomes I have experienced by staying connected to my spiritual beliefs. The internal changes I have undergone and continue to undergo are tremendous.

I have learned to focus on absolute happiness rather than relative happiness. Relative happiness is very short-lived and experienced when a desire is fulfilled. A good example of relative happiness is my night out at the nightclub with my friends back in my early twenties. I let loose, had a blast, and was deliriously joyful for the next twenty-four hours, and then the magical feeling got lost in the daily grind of life.

Absolute happiness, on the other hand, survives the worst lows of our lives. Dr. Daisaku Ikeda writes the following words in *The New Human Revolution*:

> That all our members overcome their sufferings, become healthy and enjoy comfortable lives, that they might even live in big beautiful homes and have a fine place in society, with recognition and respect—these things I wish. And, while these are certainly benefits that faith can help us attain, they are small, mediocre, compared to the ultimate benefit of faith. They are but one aspect of why we practice Buddhism.

> All we can gain from such things is relative happiness—that which never reaches beyond oneself. Our ultimate goal on the individual level is to achieve absolute happiness, to establish an indestructible palace of limitless joy in our hearts, one that will never crumble, no matter what adversity we face.

The kind of happiness we get from material things does not last forever. Therefore, we endeavor to be happy no matter what circumstances we are in. We learn not to be swayed by external influences and the people in our environment. That way, our happiness is not dependent on anything external. To achieve such a life condition is definitely no small task; it takes immense effort. But then, so does every great result. *Great results require great efforts.* There are no shortcuts.

I still have a long way to go, but I am enjoying every moment of this journey called life. My life has a purpose and a meaning, and I had to go through a lot of painful growth before realization dawned. Today, I am in the state of mind where I cherish every one of those experiences, despite the pain they caused.

My growth has not yet ended, thankfully. There is a lot of room for improvement, and that is a lifelong endeavor.

Great Results Require Great Efforts

In my younger years, I often embarked on new initiatives only to give up at the first obstacle I encountered. I would passionately throw myself into my newest obsession, thinking, "This is my life's mission." I would look for support from others and be disappointed when they weren't as enthusiastic about my plans as I was. I expected to be able to follow my dreams and that the entire universe would work around my goal. It would break my heart every time a new initiative met with failure after all the excitement I created around it for myself and everyone around me.

Today, I am consciously making an effort to overcome my impatience. In the process of reaching my objectives, I want to be happy and at peace, not restless and desperate. I am learning to make a sustained effort daily, rather than be driven by an obsessive compulsion that disappears overnight. Even so, I still fall into the same impatient trap from time to time.

My most recent obsession was to become a life coach. With all my enthusiasm, I enrolled in a course, paid over $4,000, and worked at my goal for six months. But when I had to take an exam to achieve certification, I backed off with a zillion excuses. Some days it seemed too expensive, other days I did not have time to prepare for the exams. Yet another excuse was that it took too long—all of nine months!

I have responded in exactly the same way to several other initiatives. I would take shortcuts, throw some money at the project, and look for a quick and easy way to get to my destination. Then when I failed, I would be miserable and unhappy for days. I was unclear on where I was going wrong and what I needed to change.

I have since awakened to the fact that it is ignorance that makes me think and respond with so much impatience and lack of persistence. I realize today that goals worth achieving require extraordinary effort, persistence, and courage of conviction. Time is at a premium as well. It is a challenge to do justice to a full-time job, take care of a family, and do all the activities that matter to me amidst the grind of a long list of daily errands. I used to succumb to the pressures of time and money, letting go of my dream because I did not have the gumption to fight these devils. But reading self-help books and listening to great speakers has helped me change my attitude.

One idea I have implemented successfully is journaling. Every day, I write about my feelings. I keep a notebook with me and pen down all my dreams, goals, and positive thoughts. I usually set daily goals for myself first thing each morning. Though some of the dreams and desires I write down seem impossible and others too distant, I find that the mere act of putting pen to paper makes me feel committed, as if I am making a pact with myself. I force myself to look back regularly at my jottings, because as time passes I sometimes change direction and lose track of my original destination.

Another self-improvement idea came from Matty, one of my friends in faith in Chennai. "Every time I have a negative thought," she said, "I write it down in my negativity book so I can let go of it." I began to do this too. Focusing on my attitudes, I challenge myself to overcome my shortcomings one at a time. I pour onto the pages of my notebook all the anger, helplessness, distress at being treated with disrespect, lack of faith in myself, and every other negative feeling that gets in the way of my happiness. The practice gives me helpful release from all the unhealthy emotions I experience.

I have learned to channel my anger toward becoming a woman of achievement, rather than a nitpicking, complaining, and fault-finding person. It was a slow, gradual, and often painful process for me to admit my innumerable faults. There were days when I refused to accept I was to blame for something, even when I was. But then I learned that our present circumstances (great, good, or bad) are the result of causes we have made in the past. To ensure a beautiful future we need to do our share of good deeds without fail every day. Reading and hearing the message that my life is my responsibility woke me up to reality.

It was and still is the hardest thing in the world to acknowledge that I am the cause of everything that goes wrong in my life. It was so difficult to accept I was being treated with disrespect because of causes I had made. I could no longer allow myself to think another person was wrong without first checking my own attitude and reactions. My instinct to think badly of the other person needed to be completely eradicated.

This has been the most difficult change I have had to make. Moving from thinking I was always right and that everyone else needed to change, to looking first at my own attitudes, has been a long and arduous journey. I have to draw the right balance between being a better human being and letting others take advantage of the fact that I hold myself responsible for their actions toward me. This seemed like quite a contradiction and took time to resolve itself in my head, but I am so grateful I was able to make that transition.

I am by no means a perfect or enlightened individual, but I am no longer blind to areas in my life that need improvement. Once I acknowledge a flaw in myself, I start working on it wholeheartedly. I now make a conscious effort not to speak without thinking, completely at the mercy of my feelings and thoughts, causing hurt to others by what I once called my honesty.

The biggest change within me—and one I like the most—is my "never say die" attitude. It is so much more exciting to live with an eternally positive outlook. I am not as easily affected by other people's negative words and actions anymore, and that is a wonderful benefit. I was this overly sensitive woman-child who wanted to be liked by everyone, who bent over backward trying to be in everyone's good books. I no longer pretend to be what I am not in order to be popular. I find myself being ever more true to myself; as long as I have done no wrong, then I will not let another person's judgment affect me. I combine visualization with my Buddhist practice to entrench this attitude. To prop up my self-confidence, I sometimes speak aloud to myself when I am driving or just before going to bed. For example, if I have a meeting with an antagonistic person, I tell myself, "I am calm and unaffected by this person's negative energy."

It is a delicate balance to be true to myself and at the same time have meaningful relationships. However, if I make an effort to accept people as they are and appreciate whatever they bring into their relationship with me, I will definitely attract into my life many others who feel exactly the way I do. Like every new venture in my life, my relationships need to be nurtured to realize the infinite value they have the potential of creating.

Building Community

Every year for the past nine years, I have taken a pilgrimage to be part of a larger congress of people practicing Buddhism. In India I went to a place in Delhi that felt like an oasis in the desert. A thousand members would gather there and the place would be filled with excited chatter of milestones achieved. Shining eyes, infectious laughter, and the joy of life was in the air. I always got swept away in the sea of this contagious enthusiasm.

In Canada, the conferences I attend are held in a beautiful facility in the town of Caledon, not very far from Toronto. My first meeting at Caledon was in August 2006. At that study conference, I learned from Tony Meers, who played a role in our move to Canada when we met in Japan, that Indian members in the Toronto area held their own special introductory meetings. He said approximately 250 Indians were practicing in the Toronto area.

Every time I had visited the Vancouver cultural center, my eyes had searched for familiar faces from my home country. My Buddhist leaders in India had told me about numerous members who had immigrated to Canada and were practicing there, but so far I had connected to only two Indian women. How could I connect to anymore? The rest were in Toronto!

Now I understood why, fifteen days prior to moving to Canada, I had agreed to settle in Vancouver instead of Toronto. Vancouver needed me. I was in Vancouver to represent my country and undergo hardships as an immigrant so I could support other people with similar circumstances.

I had shared very close relationships within the Buddhist community while in India. They were my friends and my family, and I had no need nor time to make other friends. Many evenings I would rush from work to a chanting session, a song rehearsal, or a study meeting. I would reach the meeting and sit down, all hunched up and feeling stressed and physically drained. My chanting was soft and lifeless at first, but by the time we concluded our prayers I was chanting loudly and vigorously, sitting up straight but calm and relaxed.

For several months after reaching Canada, I stayed in touch with members in India and continued to encourage myself through my connection with them. I sometimes missed them even more than I missed my family. But that had to change for me to progress and make Vancouver my home the way India had been. It was not so much about the place, because I loved Vancouver as a city. Its beauty enveloped me, and the people were kind too. What was missing were friends and family from my homeland. I missed people with whom I could share and chant. Several women's group members had been like sisters to me. We had shared our joys and our sorrows and together achieved milestone after milestone. If one of us was having a problem, ten others appeared out of nowhere to hold us strong. Our community and leaders had created this cohesive body of believers who were always there for one another. This was my life, my family, and I had felt complete like never before.

I will never forget when Pam, one of the women's group members in Chennai, became sick with cancer. She was the wife of Romy, a senior leader and my best friend in the practice. He was much older than me, and sometimes I thought of him as my father. I often sought his guidance. He was like a guardian angel to Jag and me, and we both trusted him greatly.

Romy was one of the first people I met when I started practicing. He would pick me up and drive me to every meeting. He was my motivation for buying a car because he was always rushing around picking up members for meetings. Invariably, we would miss the first fifteen minutes of every meeting because of this. He was a genuine, caring, and pure-hearted gentleman. He was also deeply in love with his wife, Pam, even after twenty years of marriage.

Pam had recovered from cancer once through the power of her faith and practice. She was also a great leader like Romy, very committed to her members and their well-being. She was always visiting members to encourage them. Their problems became her problems, and she attacked their issues with even more ferocity than they did themselves. I never got a chance to get very close to Pam, as she and I practiced in different areas, but I had seen and heard enough about her to have deep respect for her.

Pam shared her husband's time with all of us so generously, and Romy always admitted she was his strength. They were the perfect couple, working together to improve the world, until cancer struck again. We surrounded this couple with our prayers. While Pam was in hospital, members visited her every day and chanted silently beside her. We held relay chanting sessions across the whole city of Chennai.

When Pam passed away peacefully, her final word was "victory." But her death raised many questions among the members. She had been so sincere in her practice, one of the most compassionate women one could meet. We all struggled to understand how she could be taken from us.

I found it difficult to accept Pam's death after all my prayers; I felt doubt surging within me. I had chanted with fervent sincerity for Pam to recover. I had heard about so many people who had recovered from even more serious illnesses. Where had my prayers gone wrong? I felt inadequate and did not know how to help the grief-stricken Romy and his family. But several members appeared to support him in his moments of despair. They probably had questions too, but they put aside their personal feelings and came to stand beside Pam's husband. That was my cue to put aside my worry about myself and my inadequacy for the time being. Now was the time to be strong and help in any little way I could.

Eventually I came to understand that it isn't *when* we die that's important, but our state of mind when it happens. Chanting *Nam-myoho-renge-kyo* does not protect us from death; it provides the means to die in a peaceful state of mind, looking forward to our next life. Pam, in the final moments of her life, was showered with our prayers, and I know she felt our love. When she was gone, we all came together and took care of Romy and his family.

I was filled with pride at being part of such a humane and close-knit group of people in India, and when that support was gone after I moved to Canada, I had to rely on myself. That was good for me; I grew independent in the faith and learned to take responsibility for myself. But I also realized that someone from my country, whose faith had not had the chance to grow as mine had, could benefit from support and understanding when they arrived in Vancouver.

A new immigrant is already burdened with trying to cope with a whole new lifestyle, rebuilding a career, and dealing with one new struggle after another. Sometimes faith takes a back seat, and instead of using it to forge ahead, we get lost in the nitty-gritty of our daily existence. I had experienced that myself and wanted to help newer immigrants avoid some of my struggles. The one that had hurt the most was having to start my career from scratch, as if my fifteen years of professional experience counted for nothing. To start with an organization as a customer service executive, when I had crossed that stage several years ago, was a big blow to my professional ego. It hurt like crazy to receive no recognition of my past education or years of hard work. Every day, I yearned to return to India and ask for my old job back. I heard similar stories from several other immigrants, some of their experiences even more heartrending than Jag's and mine. Many people had to struggle for years to obtain local qualifications, investing huge amounts of time and money.

Two years after settling in Canada, I felt motivated to become an example for newer immigrants, to show them the success they could achieve if only they put their heart and soul into it. I felt inspired to become a living reminder for those who were overwhelmed to have infinite faith in their own potential.

This is what my spiritual and professional leaders in India had prepared me for when they poured their lives into guiding me. I have had the good fortune of being fostered by many great leaders, and I am the manifestation of their nurturing. I realized now was the time to follow in their footsteps, and do for others as they had done for me.

I invited an Indian women's group member I'd met in Vancouver, Sonu, to my place to chant. Both of us committed that day to welcome and support many more members from our country. Within a few months, a young men's group member, Rahul, joined us. His wife, Ria, became a dear friend much later. Soon we were also joined by Maya, a young Indian woman from Toronto. Still more members joined us in the months that followed. We have similar backgrounds and similar struggles, and that makes it easier to forge a heart-to-heart connection with each other. There is instant understanding because we have grown up with a very similar value system.

It was not always easy to connect because of the large geography of Greater Vancouver; gathering in one place was our challenge. However, we all share the vision of creating value through our Buddhist practice. We share our goals and support one another. By coming together and praying for one another, we are developing stronger bonds.

These new friendships also awakened me to the fact that a number of us arrived in Canada expecting the spiritual community to conform to our traditions and customs. But as Dr. Ikeda once said:

> When you come to another country, isn't it a mistake to compare things with Japan and expect them to be just the same? When the British or French come to Japan, I am sure they feel just as inconvenienced. Naturally, it's only human to think that there's no place like home, but, as the proverb says, "When in Rome, do as the Romans do". When we go abroad, we should try to respect and act in harmony with the cultures, values and customs of the country we are visiting. The world is getting smaller and smaller. These days, I think it is important to cultivate an international mind.

These words hit home hard. I made a conscious shift to embrace every experience and be open to new ways of doing things. I decided I would stop extolling the virtues of my birth country and resist commencing sentences with, "In India, we did . . ." If I wanted things in Vancouver to be exactly the same as they were in Chennai, I should never have left. If I failed to appreciate the opportunity to make new friends, and instead continued longing for my "friends back home," then I might as well go back. It was all in the power of my thinking—and no one could change that but me.

It has taken me a very long time to realize that the true essence of

Buddhism lies in the empowerment of the individual. Once I understood that, it was like a dam burst forth in my life. I felt like nothing could stop me from making my life exactly as I want it. It was an amazing transformation, gradual as it was.

No longer did I have to look elsewhere for abundance, beauty, joy, and prosperity. I did not have to ask anyone else because it was all already within me. I just had to bring it out and tap my highest potential. Life is beautiful, and that beauty has been revealed to me through my spiritual practice.

Moving to a new country played a crucial role in the gradual awakening that happened in my life. I began to fall in love with my adopted city, its people, and my life here. This did not mean I loved my homeland any less; it just meant that I had the good fortune of belonging to two fantastic cultures. I had the wonderful chance to bring the best from all my training in India to my new home, and I opened my life to learning as I was giving. The people in Canada had so much to teach me, if only I opened my heart and mind to them. There was no right way or wrong way of doing things; there were just different ways, and we had to keep trying until we found a way that worked for all of us.

My life in Vancouver started to take on a similar pattern as my spiritual growth in India. It became an exciting existence from one Buddhist meeting to the next. I had come full circle, and each moment brought growth, joy, and abundance with it.

Waking up to My Mission

An important lesson I learned in the initial stages of my spiritual practice was to connect my personal goals, dreams, and desires to my Buddhist practice. This has worked wonders for me.

One of the material possessions I desired in the beginning stages of my practice in India was a car. My leader, Romy, advised me to pray for a car that would carry members to and from meetings. Now, that was not quite my reason for wanting a car, but I was willing to try anything, so I went ahead and added a car to my long list of prayers. I had no idea where the money would come from or how everything would fall into place.

My dream came true within a few months—it was only a matter of redirecting my thoughts. After I started chanting about a car, I took driving lessons and obtained a driver's license. I stopped feeling overwhelmed about the cost of the car and began to take action. I researched vehicle options that would fit our budget. Jag successfully applied for a car loan and soon we were set. We bought a used car, which I drove all the time to pick up members for meetings. Prior to relocating to Canada, we sold the car to another Buddhist member. That gave me a lot of joy, as I hoped it could continue to be used to help others achieve their spiritual goals the way it had helped me.

Predictably, after this experience, every time I wanted something in life I connected it to this larger goal of world peace and happiness. For example, within the first few months of encountering Buddhism, I started hosting meetings at our place; however, it was a rented apartment. I began to pray for a larger home. As I prayed, I committed to dedicating the largest room in the house to Buddhist meetings and activities, where members could come and chant. Within a year, we bought our own home. As promised, Jag and I devoted the largest room to Buddhist activities. Other than our beautiful altar and a carpet on the floor, we kept the room empty of furniture. Our intention was to be able to accommodate as many people as possible during discussion meetings.

We lived in that beautiful home and filled it with prayer for more than four years, until we moved to Canada. As we had done with our car, we rented our home to a close friend and practitioner named Nilesh in the hope he would continue to hold Buddhist meetings there and purify our lovely home in our absence. It was our heartfelt desire that our home continue to be a place where members gather together to chant and hold Buddhist meetings.

In Canada, we moved homes four times in eighteen months, always to a bigger, nicer place. Regardless of the home we were in, we generously invited members to come and chant. We hosted meetings joyfully, and I attribute our ability to upgrade our homes to our willingness to share our space with others.

Every time I have selflessly given to others, I have received much more from the universe in return. Whether through sharing my car, my home, or just a listening ear, my most fulfilling moments are those when I am able to bring hope to other human beings. It makes me feel like I am making a difference, and that this is my purpose on this planet. Everything else is only a means to support this purpose. Giving hope to others is the reason I had to move to Vancouver, because I would not have been able to come to this realization if I had not moved. Although deep down I know my life was building toward this purpose since the first time I chanted *Nam-myoho-renge-kyo*, I had to travel thousands of miles to truly understand my mission and have the courage to follow my heart.

As Lisa Nichols, featured teacher in the book *The Secret* says, "You have come to this juncture in your life, merely because something in you kept saying, 'You deserve to be happy.' You were born to add something, to add value to this world. To simply being something, bigger and better than you were yesterday."

I have spoken so much about *Nam-myoho-renge-kyo* being my grounding reality, but more recently I came to understand that I needed to invite abundance into my life by watching *The Secret*. I was so motivated by the message of this movie that I bought the unabridged versions of the CDs. My heart races every time I hear Bob Doyle, Lisa Nichols, and many other great speakers share with firm conviction about the power of attracting abundance into one's life. I do not agree with every word of *The Secret*, but the prime point of inviting what we want in our lives by maintaining a positive attitude and recognizing that our thoughts become our reality resonated within me.

Another well-known personality who has affected me is Oprah. I got hooked watching her show after moving to Vancouver. She has created immense value in my life. I felt empowered through her discussions about weight management, abuse toward women and children, and the achievements of ordinary human beings. Through her shows, I also heard about Eckhart Tolle; his book, *A New Earth*, has had tremendous impact on my life and relationships.

Without the wisdom and open-mindedness I have obtained through chanting *Nam-myoho-renge-kyo*, I doubt I could have applied the knowledge of these inspiring individuals to propel my life forward. Yes, the material benefits in my life have been much appreciated, but the most beautiful and valuable gift I have received has been unshakeable confidence in myself and my abilities. I finally understand that each of us has boundless power, imagination, creativity, and courage to achieve our desires. The human mind has a glorious, limitless ability to bring forth all that it can visualize.

I believe I have also gained protection from mental stress and physical challenges, including serious accidents. In April 2008, I was driving down a street when another car came out of a driveway and hit my vehicle on the passenger side with such force that my car swerved into the next lane. I lost control and ended up hitting a fence and a huge wooden pole. The front of my vehicle was completely smashed in from the impact. Before I could even gather what happened, the street was swarmed with police cars, screaming ambulances, and a fire truck racing down the road toward me.

I was helped out of my car and checked for broken bones. Although my back hurt like crazy, I suffered not a single visible scratch. My car was a different story; it was a total write-off and had to be replaced by the insurance company. A month after the accident, I was hit once again by another driver making a left turn out of sequence at an uncontrolled intersection. This aggravated my back pain and my brand new car had to be towed into the repair shop. My immune system weakened after the accidents and I suffered severe breathing-related concerns, sinusitis, and allergies, but I was able to overcome these problems.

The biggest health milestone I have achieved was to rid my body of an addiction to nasal drops. I was addicted to this medication for almost twenty years. One of my doctors referred to it as my emotional crutch. When I first heard this, my instant reaction was to deny it. However, as I reflected about my doctor's words over the next few days, I began to see the sense in them.

Reality hit me in the face, penetrating my denial as I started to observe that the moment I was anxious or fearful, my breathing became constricted and I automatically reached into my bag for the nasal drops. Like a person obsessed, I would continue to pour more drops down my nose every few minutes, even though it was decreasingly effective. The less it helped, the more I used, and the more I used, the more harm I caused to myself. Over two decades of use, I damaged my nasal passages to the point that I could not live a normal life. The simple act of breathing, which most human beings take for granted, became a huge effort for me. There were days when I used the drops every five hours, and at night it got even worse. My breathing affected me to the point that I couldn't sleep for more than three hours at a stretch without waking up in desperation, looking for that bottle. I despised my helplessness, but I was so weak. Whenever I tried to stop using the spray, I began to feel choked and claustrophobic. It was scary to be so dependent on something.

The conversation with my doctor directed my attention to the fact that I had an addiction. I recoiled at the very thought that I was addicted to something. I had seen firsthand with my father the effects of addiction and I didn't want any part of it, yet here I was living that reality myself. It took me several weeks of self-reflection before I was able to uncover the patterns in my life and really accept my addiction as an indisputable fact.

For the first time in my life, I understood how my dad must have struggled. I could see so clearly now why my voice must not have been reaching him when I cried and pleaded with him to stop drinking. Jag tried several times to get me off the drops, and I promised him every time that I would stop, but I always succumbed to the vice.

The most unbelievable aspect is that I accepted and lived with the issue until January 2009, when I added it to my resolutions for the year. Within three months, thanks to prayer and the help of my family doctor, I finally cured myself of the addiction. It required courage, my prayers, and all my willpower to achieve this. I held on to these lines from a book, *The Buddha in Daily Life*:

> The healing process begins with strengthening the confidence with which you can say to yourself: "I can defeat my sickness. I can change the poison in my body into medicine." If our condition of being is one of defeat, sickness will defeat our will to heal. If it is one of challenge, then we have maximized the possibility of recovery.

Physical, emotional, financial, and spiritual: I want the best life possible in all these aspects. After praying consistently to live a life free of complaints, grudges, and regrets, I am slowly but surely learning to do that. As I chant, I become stronger mentally and am guided to take the right actions. I am no longer a puppet at the mercy of what the people around me think, say, and do. I have accepted that I have little control over others. My words, even though spoken with the best intentions, do not always penetrate the lives of the people I care about. The only things within my control are my feelings, thoughts, words, and actions, and it is an exhilarating sensation to be in complete charge of that.

Evolution

That child who had retreated into her shell completely, who allowed herself to believe she could not be happy, prosperous, or successful, is a distant memory, a ghost of the past. Earlier in my life, I mastered the art of hiding my feelings and retreating within myself instead of living it up. I was living a facade, afraid to share my deepest self with even my own family. I did not understand it then, but my newfound wisdom tells me I did not expect the real me to be loved or wanted, so I played different roles and tried to be what others expected in order to win them over. *Nam-myoho-renge-kyo* shook my life to the core and unearthed all the beauty and joy within me that was crying out to be shared.

Such was the extent of lack of faith in my own worth, that for several years I even doubted my parents' love for me. I believed they loved my elder sister, Sangeeta, more than they loved me. This adversely affected my interactions with Sangeeta. I would not express myself freely for fear of letting her know that I felt unloved, and I held her responsible for taking away what was rightfully mine. I carried this with me until Sangeeta and her two children visited me in Vancouver in 2008.

I made a shift during that visit, and cursed myself for letting so many years pass without reaching out to her. What a terrible mess I had made with all my emotional confusion! When we were growing up together, my sister loved me and protected me like a mother. Even today, she is like a fierce tigress with a cub if she senses I am unhappy with something or someone. How could I have forgotten that?

How much insecurity, misconception, anger, mistrust, and other negative emotions I was living with. Reading Eckhart Tolle's book, *A New Earth*, woke me to the ego within my own life that was consuming my happiness. It also alerted me to my uncontrolled responses to other people. Above all, it allowed me to break free of my limited span of thinking where complex family relationships are concerned. Tolle says:

> Whatever you think people are withholding from you—praise, appreciation, assistance, loving care, and so on—give it to them. You don't have it? Just act as if you had it, and it will come. Then soon after you start giving, you will start receiving. You cannot receive what you don't give. Outflow determines inflow.

It no longer matters whether Sangeeta was loved more than me or not; even if she was, it was not her fault. The past is beyond repair, but my present and my future matter. For my own sanity and happiness, I had to learn to let go of all the baggage I was carrying around for years on end.

After Sangeeta and her family left for India, I missed them terribly, and slipped back into feeling the loneliness I felt upon first moving to Canada. After a very long period of positivity, I suddenly felt unenthusiastic and wanted to stay in my comfort zone, without having to extend myself. I found it hard to sit down and chant as my passion for Buddhism receded to the background.

This was not the first time I had gone through this kind of setback, so as difficult as it was, I kept chanting in my heart from time to time, searching for a way to get back in rhythm.

Thankfully, I was revived by a visit to the Florida Nature and Cultural Center (FNCC) for a Buddhist conference in September 2008. Every presenter spoke with such sincere passion that not one person was unmoved. The women's leader spoke for one and a half hours, and I was awed by her amazing energy, passion, and commitment. Every word pierced my heart and my life. She talked as if she were speaking from the depth of her being, as if she realized she had to make the most of this opportunity to help others realize the changes they sought in their lives. Her session extended late into the night, until 12:30 a.m. I was tired and exhausted, but she seemed as fresh as she had in the morning and looked like she could go on forever. Her compassion was selfless, powerful, and palpable.

The part of her message that I embedded into my heart was that our lives are a daily struggle with the negativity within us, and it is up to us whether the negativity wins or we do. Negativity can come from within in the form of anger, lethargy, arrogance, depression, and so on, or it can originate from outside through a specific person or situation. The prime reason we chant *Nam-myoho-renge-kyo* is because it is so hard for us to stay positive all the time. I understood that so clearly, especially in the face of the lethargy and sadness I had been feeling since Sangeeta's departure. The women's leader's words made me aware that such negativity is a part of all our lives, and I was not the only one fighting this constantly. Enlightenment is a lifelong journey, not a destination. Problems are the fuel for making the journey more exciting.

I wanted to do everything possible while at the conference. It was an opportunity to deepen my understanding of life. I was awed by some of the struggles people had overcome through the power of their Buddhist practice. In particular, the immense courage of one comrade in faith, Sanjeev, had a big impact on me.

Sanjeev spoke about his desire to own an airline. Just the thought of having such a huge idea scared me—forget about making it actually happen. Besides the fear that held me back from dreaming so big, I was always afraid of looking foolish in front of my friends if I was not able to make my dreams a reality. But this young man obviously had no such inhibitions. I was dumbstruck by Sanjeev's courage and his passionate resolve. I felt inspired, and at the same time envied his courage to stand up in a room full of people and speak with complete conviction. It was incredible. I tried to visualize doing that myself, and had goose pimples from the fear. But it makes complete sense to me now to do that. If I make a commitment I am more likely to work toward it, so it is definitely important to voice it. And who better to share it with than those who support me with their prayers?

I was truly encouraged by the spirit of this young man with his vision of an airline. There was no arrogance or boastfulness in his simple statement, only pure conviction. The youth present at the meeting were obviously as inspired as I was, because they gathered around Sanjeev afterward, and all of them made a shared determination to return to the same conference the following year to report their victories.

I prayed for all of them. As a woman and a mother, it is clear to me these young people are the ones who will secure the peace and happiness of our land if we guide them correctly. I believe that if I support the youth, the good causes I make will become a benefit for my own children. Maybe not today, maybe not tomorrow, but whenever they need them, protective forces will appear in response to all the positive energy I create. Buddhism promises us that our actions will affect the seven generations before us and the seven generations after us. That is the power of our prayer and the positive causes we make throughout our lives.

The Florida conference was a life-transforming experience for me. On my way back to Vancouver, I was in a highly reflective state of mind. I went through all my notes from the conference so I could create an updated list of goals. I knew that I wished to contribute in a very tangible way to changing my world, but I did not yet know how I was going to do that.

Weeks after returning home, the "how" continued to evade me because I was using my mind, not my heart. I was constantly strategizing, planning, and working my mind into a frenzy, but it was not helping. I reminded myself that as long as I allowed the *how* to dominate my thoughts, my path would remain unclear. If I could just stay with the picture of what I wanted and feel the passion throbbing within my heart, the how would clarify itself. This was a learning from *The Secret*, where Rhonda Byrne quotes Martin Luther King: "Take the first step in faith. You don't have to see the whole staircase. Just take the first step." It was imperative for me to focus on *what* I wanted, rather than the how, because the how deflated all my energy and diffused my enthusiasm. That is what finally worked. I wrote down my goal—to create value in the lives of others through my written communication skills—and looked at it as many times a day as possible.

As I set about realizing my goal, I took several detours along the way, experimenting with different options: simply blogging, writing for a magazine, and so on. I wanted to find a way to create a stream of heart-to-heart connections and bring people together through the written word. There were several times when I thought, "This is it!" only to have things not work out. Despite those missteps, my first effort at writing emerged. I wrote two chapters of a self-help book titled *Your Victory Is My Victory*. That theme resonated with me strongly, because that is what Buddhism clearly expresses. It is all about creating a win-win situation for everyone; it is about rejoicing in the victories of the people around us.

It was a struggle to write that book. All the lessons I had learned during my ten years of Buddhist practice were vying to be expressed, and my words would not flow. I was disguising Buddhist principles and trying to express them as motivational management concepts. I failed in my attempt and could not carry on.

The night I made the decision to scrap that book, I felt like a failure, someone who lacked grit, determination, and courage. I felt completely crushed and just sat in front of my laptop, staring at the screen blindly for hours. Jag was away at a conference in Caledon, and I had no one to share my sorrow with. That night was exactly ten years from the day I had first chanted *Nam-myoho-renge-kyo*.

The next day, I bowed my head in sincere prayer in front of my altar, and within twenty-four hours, *Journey in Faith* was born. I wrote the first page of this book on October 17, 2008. From another deep sorrow, once again, my prayers had given me complete clarity and greater joy. It is only through my own life that I can express how powerful Buddhism is. I have shared my experiences innumerable times in the past ten years, and now I am bringing them all together. My intention is to gift the compilation to my mentor, Dr. Daisaku Ikeda, as a way of expressing my gratitude to him for the inspiration he has been in my life. No matter how many times I say, "Thank you, Sensei," it will never be enough.

The Joy of Buddhism

Writing this book has given me a new reason to wake up each morning. As Josei Toda writes in *The New Human Revolution*, "Knowing your mission means you have found something for which you would gladly give your life without regrets."

I am not yet willing to give up my life, because I have never felt happier about being alive. I look forward to the time each day that I have dedicated to writing. Life has taken on a whole new perspective. My faith has definitely reached the point of no return, as I like to call it.

With my writing, I hope to inspire others to find their own unique path, one that gives them as much meaning as I have found in Buddhism and leads them to winning lives in which they keep going no matter how difficult their present situation may be. This brings to mind a much-loved song from India called "I seek Sensei," with the words "never give up." My friend Matty, whose idea of the negativity book I adopted, is a professional singer, and this was the first song she professionally recorded for the community. I have been inspired by it on many occasions when I have been at my lowest ebb.

After moving to Vancouver, I listened to the song every morning while driving my car. I would sing along with Matty and feel my spirits lifting. At other times, tears would flow, and I would get emotional at the lines, "No matter what, I'll surely win, never give up, never give in!" During my darkest days, her beautiful voice gave me the courage to go on. Every time I was tempted to give up, I would listen to these words and find the courage to strive for the best. Her voice gave me hope and forced me to take action and move forward.

At the FNCC conference, a cultural evening took place on the last day. A large group of fifteen young women's group members took the stage and began singing, "I Seek Sensei." I was so excited that I jumped out of my chair, clapping and singing even louder than the performers. It was an emotional moment for me, and I guess everyone else was touched too, because soon the whole audience was dancing to the song. The young woman who led the song shared with me later that Matty had once said she had read nine volumes of *The New Human Revolution* series before attempting to sing this song. Having been in Chennai with Matty when she recorded the song, I was surprised to learn this fact. Yet again, Matty had inspired me.

I decided to tear a page from her book and study *The New Human Revolution* with my friends Aruna and Ria. We began to study line by line and as often as possible. Aruna was the answer to my prayers when my family and I moved from Vancouver to the nearby city of Richmond. She moved from Delhi, India, straight into the community in early 2008 after marrying an Indian gentleman in Vancouver. Both Ria and Aruna have deep faith that is pure and sincere.

We meet often and chant together, sharing our lives with one another and supporting the cause of world peace and happiness in our own unique ways. Despite the fact that they were both newly married, Aruna and Ria always had time for chanting and Buddhist study. It is truly satisfying to watch these lovely women bloom and awaken to the beauty of their own lives.

Being a Buddhist leader (a position I was appointed to two years after beginning my spiritual practice in India) has been a blessing I am truly appreciative of. Where else would I have had the opportunity to grasp so many principles of leadership? I was able to apply all of these lessons at work as a manager of people, as well as at home as a mother of two children. These lessons taught me how to work with people of different backgrounds and diverse upbringing.

I have also learned how to forge my character and live with courage and dignity. Sometimes I am very hard on myself, because I have been told time and again that only I can change my life. I am the one responsible every time someone does not treat me well. I am the one who has made causes when my environment is gloomy and people are unforgiving and lacking in compassion. Buddhism has taught me that since I have made the causes, only I can change the effects. I can do this by practicing correctly and by consciously making good causes, and the best way to do that is to help others grow to be capable leaders so they in turn can foster more capable leaders. The bigger the team, the more we can achieve, and the whole journey becomes so much more exciting.

Leadership is not just about increasing the size of our spiritual community. It is about spreading peace, joy, and harmony, and creating value for humanity—and having fun while doing all of that. Undeniably, success is an automatic by-product in the lives of those who help others to be successful. Because we have the treasure of a life-transforming faith, it's our privilege to share and expand the sphere of compassion, joy, and laughter as much as we can. Our power to do this is significant. We are restricted only by thoughts that do not comprehend how much difference a single human being can make. Dr. Ikeda says, "A great human revolution in just a single individual will enable the change in the destiny of all humankind."

I did not think like this until Buddhism happened to me. Just as Buddhism taught me to take responsibility for all the negative aspects of my life, so have I learned that I have immense potential; each one of us does. I use Buddhism to help me tap that potential. Every time I need to be uplifted in spirit or physical energy, *Nam-myoho-renge-kyo* is my source.

In my next lifetime I wish to be born as a "fortune baby." A fortune baby is a child born to parents who are already practicing Buddhism when the baby is born. In this birth, I lost out on years of opportunity to practice because I encountered Buddhism after I was married and had a baby. Not that I have any regrets; I am more than making up for the lost time.

I have received great joy from taking on all kinds of roles at every Buddhist meeting. Sometimes I take my turn at the front, but it gives me as much pleasure to work backstage. It all depends on the members I am working with, their strengths, and what gives them joy in the practice. I can contribute in innumerable ways, and though I learned to enjoy taking center stage when required, I am happy to welcome people at the door too.

That is another aspect I received training in. I used to be quite shy to stand on stage, but now I am very comfortable in front of a microphone. It is a great benefit to have been able to enhance my public speaking skills, and being forced to take center stage pushed me toward studying and better understanding Buddhism. Study has been instrumental in helping to deepen my faith and practice correctly. If I do not study, I am unable to obtain the best results out of my practice. If I have this powerful tool in my hand but I don't know how to use it, what good is it to me?

Often when I am facing a difficult situation or challenge, I will find the exact motivation I need to take action. This happens so frequently that it never ceases to amaze me. Just when I reach the limits of my endurance, a message comes to me either through a book, a friend, or sometimes inner wisdom. Buddhism has been the springboard for finding the connection between challenge and solution.

For me, Buddhism is practical and it is reason. Prayer is the starting point; everything else follows. Whenever I have a desire or a goal, I often find I am initially unclear about how I will make it happen; the bigger the goal, the less clarity in my case. So I just write it down and chant about it. As I chant, ideas and thoughts come to me and my creativity gets activated. I start to take action based on those ideas. People emerge and circumstances change to help me make my dream a reality. It's like everything starts to align with my dreams. Sometimes this alignment takes a few days, and in some cases it has taken me years, depending on my focus and commitment toward the goal, and how much good fortune I have accumulated in my life.

My life has become so abundant over the past few years. My children have everything that I never had as a kid: their own rooms, bicycles, fancy toys, laptop computers, and so on. As I focused on making my dreams come true, my life opened in ways I could never have imagined.

I don't want to misguide you. Chanting does not guarantee that life will be a bed of roses. What it does guarantee is that even when there are innumerable thorns in our path, we can still look at the roses and smile. That, to me, is more important than anything else. I pray to live a life of abundance: spiritual, emotional, and financial, in that order. Chanting helps to bring out the beauty and happiness within.

Over the past few years I have been able to accomplish so many things that mattered to me. Music was one of those things I had allowed to slip away. As a little girl, I wanted to learn to play the piano. I took some lessons when I was in Grade 7, but the music teacher lived quite far from our home; it took me an hour to walk back and forth. What's more, we could not afford a piano, so I did not have a chance to practice between lessons. True to my character, I gave up. Another dream faded into nothingness.

Being part of a spiritual community where there is constant appreciation of music, art, and culture has rekindled my love for music. I don't have a very melodious voice, but what I lack in tone and rhythm I make up for in effort and passion. Today, Reyna and I both attend piano lessons, and Jag recently bought me a digital piano so I can practice.

I want to light the world in any which way I can. No longer do I stop myself from dreaming or sharing my dreams. I may realize some dreams sooner than others, and may change my mind about some completely. I learned from the young man, Sanjeev, who expressed his airline ambition at the FNCC conference. His courage to share something so big gave me the courage to share my dreams and goals as well, as long as I did so with the same humility he showed.

Looking back at all the times I made the effort of writing my experiences down and sharing my thoughts at a meeting, I realize I was unconsciously enhancing my communication skills. Soon I was helping others to edit their experiences, which in turn made me a better communicator. This was not planned; I did it because it made me happy, and it unearthed a skill I had not even thought much about. In the long run, the help I extended to others benefited me more than them. It increased my eloquence in speaking, and helped me structure my flow of thoughts while writing. This was clearly the law of cause and effect at work yet again.

Afterword

At the end of every Buddhist discussion, a member who is sharing his or her experience thanks everyone for their patient listening. I need to do that too. Regardless of whether you have been able to read every page or just some portions, I want to thank you for taking the time.

Some new aspects of Buddhism may have opened up for you as you read, or maybe you already knew most of the concepts and I was able to help refresh some forgotten principles. Either way, I truly hope you have enjoyed my words.

In case you are seeking to know a little more about Nichiren Buddhism, several online resources are available. One of my personal favorites is a YouTube clip of Tina Turner in an interview with Larry King, where she speaks about her experience with Buddhism. There are also many resources for new members on the SGI-USA website.

Regardless of whether one is a Buddhist or not, the future of our world depends on each and every one of us. That is no small responsibility. Though we cannot all be prime ministers and presidents, we each have our own part to play on the grand stage of world peace and happiness. Everyone has different strengths and can contribute in their unique way. We can impact our neighborhoods, cities, countries—the whole world—if we so choose.

I am making that choice today, at this very moment. Will you make it with me?

Let's all stand together and promise to create value, make a difference, and prove the immense power of a single human being. Let the world see and feel that we are dedicated to its safety. What are we waiting for? Let's exploit our individual differences and use our unique strengths and talents to do what we were born to do. Not for a moment can we forget the realities of life and our day-to-day existence, but surely, in a twenty-four-hour day, we can take half an hour to pray for ourselves, our loved ones, and strangers we have never even met. That in itself is a contribution to humanity. If thirty minutes is difficult, start with five or ten minutes and then work your way up, minute by minute, day by day.

When we pray, we activate our wisdom and motivation to do more for others. We will all have varying degrees of effect, and so be it. Whether we reach one person or a hundred, our cause is common. We are united in our ultimate goal of world peace and happiness. We may not be able to speak to world leaders or hold dialogues with famous personalities about our cause, but surely we can speak to the person sitting next to us at work, or our best friend with whom we have lunch every day.

If each of us plays our part based on our own creativity and different strengths, we can create a heaven within our own communities. We can spread the message of love, peace, happiness, and unity, creating a ripple effect that will reach the other end of the world. We can make the hurt and the pain we experience into our salvation. Every obstacle can be turned into an opportunity.

I firmly believe there is no such thing as failure. Failures are a series of detours we make to reach a life more beautiful than our best dreams. The more I resisted the pain and the hardships of my life, the weaker I became. But when I looked them in the eye and made it clear I was going to take them on, they just slithered away with their tails between their legs. Instead of becoming weaker, I grew in strength.

Regardless of my past and the circumstances I grew up in, the choice is mine to allow those lessons to make me a better human being. Rather than wallow in self-pity, cursing the fact that I have not had the opportunities of some of my friends, I can glow like the beautiful lotus flower that blooms in the swamp—but I have to make the choice to glow.

Please do your best where you are now, and have no regrets.

Appreciating the present moment can help you live a joy-filled future, not only for yourself but for all humanity. Start with this moment, in any little way you can. Do one thing every single day to encourage another person or bring a smile to a troubled friend. Our good intentions will penetrate the universe.

I cannot conclude without offering my sincere appreciation to Bharat Soka Gakkai (India) and SGI Canada, as well as all the senior leaders, especially Tony Meers and Cindy Kaufman, who are supporting my initiative. I give my heartfelt appreciation to everyone I have mentioned in the book, and thank them for their permission to use my interactions with them.

And of course, Jag, Aman, and Reyna: this book would never have been possible without your unconditional love and support.

In all humility, I must say that I owe my current existence and joy in life to my Buddhist practice. Through the power of my faith and through practice and study, I have sometimes moved forward inch by inch and sometimes raced toward my dreams at top speed. Month after month, year after year, I am striving to become a better human being tomorrow than I was today or yesterday. Through the victories I achieve in my life, I will show actual proof of the power of faith. I might be a small drop in the vast ocean of humanity, but I can create a stream that will support the river of global harmony and purify the sea of humanity.

Bibliography and Additional Reading

Allen, James (2005). *As a Man Thinketh*. New Delhi, India: Sterling Publishers.

Byrne, Rhonda (2006). *The Secret*. New York: Atria Books.

Causton, Richard (1995). *The Buddha in Daily Life: Introduction to the Buddhism of Nichiren Daishonin*. London: Arrow Books.

Daishonin, Nichiren (1999). *The Writings of Nichiren Daishonin*. Tokyo: Soka Gakkai.

Hochswende, Woody, & Morino, Greg (2001). *The Buddha in Your Mirror*. U.S.A.: Middleway Press.

Izzo, John (2008). *The Five Secrets You Must Discover Before You Die*. San Francisco: Berrett-Koehler Publishers.

Sharma, Robin (2006). *The Greatness Guide*. Ontario: HarperCollins.

Tolle, Eckhart (2005). *A New Earth*. New York: Penguin.

Dr. Daisaku Ikeda's books:
Before It Is Too Late with Aurelio Peccei
Buddhism, the First Millenium
The Cherry Tree (children's book)
Choose Life: A Dialogue with Arnold J. Toynbee
Choose Peace with Johan Galtung
Dawn after Dark with René Huyghe
Dialogical Civilization with Tu Weiming

A Dialogue between East and West: Looking to a Human Revolution with Ricardo Diez-Hochleitner

Dialogue of World Citizens with Norman Cousins

Faith into Action

The Flower of Chinese Buddhism

For the Sake of Peace

Global Civilization: A Buddhist-Islamic Dialogue with Majid Tehranian

Human Values in a Changing World with Bryan Wilson

Humanity at the Crossroads with Karan Singh

Kanta and the Deer (children's book)

Life: An Enigma, a Precious Jewel

A Lifelong Quest for Peace with Linus Pauling

The Living Buddha

Moral Lesson of the Twentieth Century with Mikhail Gorbachev

My Recollections

The New Human Revolution (ten volumes)

On Peace, Life and Philosophy with Henry Kissinger

One by One

Over the Deep Blue Sea (children's book)

Planetary Citizenship with Hazel Henderson

The Princess and the Moon (children's book)

A Quest for Global Peace: Rotblat and Ikeda on War, Ethics, and the Nuclear Threat with Joseph Rotblat

Revolutions: To Green the Environment, to Grow the Human Heart with M.S. Swaminathan

The Snow Country Prince (children's book)

Songs of Peace: Rendezvous with Nature (Photographs)

Toward Creating an Age of Humanism with John Kenneth Galbraith

Unlocking the Mysteries of Birth and Death: A Buddhist View of Life

The Way of Youth: Buddhist Common Sense for Handling Life's Questions (with a foreword by Duncan Sheik)

The Wisdom of the Lotus Sutra (six volumes)

A Youthful Diary